NED WAYBURN AND THE DANCE ROUTINE

NED WAYBURN AND THE DANCE ROUTINE

From Vaudeville to the *Ziegfeld Follies*

Barbara Stratyner

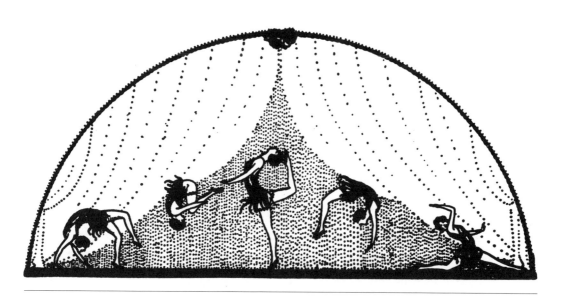

STUDIES IN DANCE HISTORY, NO. 13
SOCIETY OF DANCE HISTORY SCHOLARS
1996

Published by The Society of Dance History Scholars.

Printed in the United States of America by A-R Editions, Madison, Wisconsin.

ISSN 1043 7592

ISBN 0-9653519-2-0

Library of Congress Catalog Card Number 96-070657

COVER ART: Scene from *Ned Wayburn's Symphonic Jazz Revue*, 1924. Ned Wayburn, *The Art of Stage Dancing* (1925), p. 93.

TITLE PAGE ART: Line art from Ned Wayburn, *The Art of Stage Dancing* (1925), p. 103.

PAGE 62 ART: Line art from Ned Wayburn, *The Art of Stage Dancing* (1925), p. 7.

Contents

List of Illustrations   vii

Preface   ix

Early Life and Influences   1

Dance Idioms and Performance Hierarchies   14

Vaudeville Feature Acts   21

Individual Specialty Acts   33

Chorus Specialty Acts   51

Conclusion   60

Notes   63

Selected Chronology of Shows Staged by Ned Wayburn   73

Ned Wayburn's Notated Dance Instructions   82

    "Home-Study Course in Stage Dancing"   83

      "Foundation Technique" (Lessons 1-5)   84

      "Ballet Technique" (Lessons 41-45)   91

    "Acrobatic High Kicking Routine"   98

    "The Savannah Stomp"   100

    "Ned Wayburn's Ballroom Charleston"   102

    "The Original 'Footloose' Strut"   106

Bibliography   107

Index   121

Students in Wayburn's "foundation course" performing sit-ups
and rollovers at his New York studio, ca. 1923.   3

The eight directions of Wayburn's "compass."   7

Instructions for a march for sixteen performers.   9

Cartoon by W.C. Fields, 1920.   12

Evelyn Law in the final movement of a hitch kick.   15

Virginia Bacon in an acrobatic ballet pose.   17

Types of shoes recommended for use at the Ned Wayburn studio
in the 1920s.   19

The Phantastic Phantoms (1907).   23

Ned Wayburn's Minstrel Misses (1902).   27

Corene Uzell (left) and Julia Lamaedrid in "In Old Mexico,"
The Daisy Dancers (1906).   29

Rosalia Ceballos working the double rings in the Act II opening
scene of *The Midnight Sons* (1909).   34

An X-ray of Mazie King's foot and ankle with photographs showing
her in poses from an eccentric ballet solo, 1899.   39

Carter de Haven and Fred Nice, Jr., in "rube" outfits, performing
tandem mirror work and shadowing work.   41

Jack Donahue and Evelyn Law in the final pose of an eccentric
whirlwind in *Two Little Girls in Blue* (1921).   43

Madeleine and Marion Fairbanks taking a curtain call for
"A Miniature," *Ziegfeld Follies of 1918*.   47

John Parks and chorus in "My Little Havana Made,"
The Wife Hunters (1911).   52

"A-dancers" or show girls in costume for the *Ziegfeld Follies of 1922*.   57

Dolores as the White Peacock, *Ziegfeld Midnight Frolics*, 1919.   59

The dance direction of musical shows in the opening decades of the twentieth century has long been ignored by both theater and dance historians. The study of choreography during these years, however, can reveal the sources of many elements that are still used in live, film, and broadcast entertainment.

The seminal element developed in this period was the routine. A structure for solo, team, and chorus performance, it was the offspring of theatrical necessity. Growing out of nineteenth-century ballet extravaganzas and influenced by theater architecture and popular music, the routine was essential to Wayburn's dance direction and choreography.

This study began as a joint professional biography of the three women who received "stager" or dance director credits in the opening five years of this century—Aida Overton Walker, Gertrude Hoffmann, and Dorothy Marlowe. Although their careers as performers and choreographers were easily documented, there was little detailed information about the actual content of their routines and other dances. The decision was thus made to analyze the work of a single, astonishingly prolific dance director, Ned Wayburn, who left abundant documentation both of his career and the specifics of his routines and dances—perhaps the most complete body of material for any choreographer in the commercial theater. Wayburn worked in musical comedies, revues, vaudeville feature acts, Prologs, silent feature films, and early television, as well as producing for radio. He employed all the movement vocabularies of the period—native American tap, exhibition ballroom dances, musical comedy styles, and such European imports as ballet, acrobatics, and national dances. To all these media and vocabularies, Wayburn brought an invaluable sense of rhythm, a unique ability to invent new paths of movement, and a deep understanding of the proscenium stage.

In the sixteen years since the dissertation on which this book is based was written, the study of dance history and the study of dance as an element of theater history have grown and changed. The work that follows is a structural analysis, a methodology used in the late 1970s for analyzing postmodern dance and popular entertainments. This approach easily lent itself to documenting the individual movements, routines, and stage pictures found in Wayburn's choreography.[1]

Crucially important to his work was a concern for spatial organization and the sensory relationship with the audience established by the arrangement of performers onstage. All of Wayburn's choreography, and that of Walker, Hoffmann, Marlowe, and their contemporaries, was conceived for an audience seated in front of the stage curtain, and some of his most innovative creations involved experiments in handling the space of a traditional proscenium stage. Equally important to his work was the shared knowledge that connected it to the public. The timing and success of a Wayburn routine depended on the audience comprehending an allusion—getting the joke. These jokes could be conveyed in the spoken dialogue or sung lyrics or presented as a visual reference, or "sight gag." Frequently, Wayburn's construction of a long production number depended entirely on the audience's knowledge of contemporary entertainment. Since, today, allusions to New York politics of the 1910s or consumer products of the 1920s are apt to be unfamiliar, I have supplied such information either in the body of the text or in the endnotes. With one major exception, all the large-scale production numbers that I analyze relate to dance history and personalities.

Wayburn thrived in a commercial theater that was created by and for profit-making businessmen. Most of his work as a dance director was created for profit-oriented producers—Marc Klaw and A.L. Erlanger, Lew Fields, the Shubert Brothers, Charles B. Dillingham, Florenz Ziegfeld, Jr.—and their white male financial backers. Wayburn himself was frequently involved in financial as well as artistic partnerships with these producers. This was the theater he knew, and he did his best work for it.

Wayburn's feature acts in vaudeville were aimed at family audiences and couples, but the target audience for many of his revues was male. The roof garden acts that he created during summer seasons, the Lew Fields musicals, and the *Ziegfeld Midnight Frolics* attracted an almost exclusively male audience. In analyzing various routines, this study documents how material was targeted to that audience, which had tastes and interests that, by our standards, were sexist and/or racist. Wayburn's fascination with the minstrel shows of his childhood in the 1880s was expressed overtly in his feature act *Ned Wayburn's Minstrel Misses*, where the cast "blacked up" onstage, as well as in the entrance parades that he used throughout his career. His innovative work for Lew Fields's summer shows was aimed at "summer widowers," businessmen whose families spent the months of July and August in the country. The stunning finale of the *Passing Show of 1912* was a parody of the suffragist movement that layered negative allusions to women and feminists into spoken and sung texts, character names, and visual references. "It's Getting Darker on Broadway," a chorus production number, incorporated some of the most racist material in any Wayburn/Ziegfeld show into a complaint that African American revues were "taking over" Broadway.

Because at the outset of his career Wayburn had been both an architectural draftsman and a professional musician, and because he continued to design sets and write songs, one can study his dances in relation to all aspects of musical comedy staging. It is possible to learn how he adapted movement to the physical limitations of a set or manipulated techniques to fit the rhythms of contemporary ragtime and jazz. As Wayburn was also a teacher and the founding manager of a number of dance studios, one can also analyze actual dances and examples of his codified techniques. Notations for some of his lessons and routines are reprinted at the end of this book.

Two problems presented themselves in studying Wayburn's career. The first was the sheer volume of his work: each of his more than three hundred shows and two hundred acts included at least four dance numbers. One obvious solution to this problem was to limit the study to numbers involving dance—a decision that eliminated comics like Eddie Cantor, W.C. Fields, Al Jolson, and Will Rogers. Another solution was to keep the number of examples to a minimum.

The second problem was caused by Wayburn himself. Like many directors and performers of his time, he had a tendency to exaggerate, mislead, or prevaricate in advertisements and interviews. Since so much material comes from advertising brochures and promotional articles, this habit presented major difficulties. Every statement made by Wayburn, and every credit claimed by him, has been checked and corroborated by three independent sources of the period. I have been fairly conservative in accepting his statements. While it is possible that Wayburn staged the original New York *Floradora*, taught Will Rogers to twirl a lasso, put Eddie Cantor and Al Jolson in blackface, and invented the industrial show, I am not wholly persuaded that any of these claims are true.

Although this study uses the vocabularies of theater, dance, and music, an attempt has been made to clarify the language. All words such as "routine" or "step" that had a specific meaning for Wayburn, but signify something quite different to the contemporary reader, have been explained the first time they are used. Certain words and phrases with multiple meanings have been avoided. For example, "chorus" will be used to designate a group of dancers only, not the middle section of a popular song (which will be called a refrain).

This book has been researched almost entirely from newspaper articles preserved in clipping, production, or personality files and scrapbooks. Most of the reviews and promotional articles cited in the text can only be identified by periodical, date, subject of scrapbook or file, and collection: authors and titles are seldom indicated. Since so little has been written on the subject, I believe that even these incomplete citations provide essential information and should be used.

The other major sources have been scripts, set and costume designs, and music for each of the 150 Wayburn shows I have studied in detail. Most of the scripts, all of the manuscript music (primarily orchestral parts), and many of the printed songs come from the Shubert Archives or private collections. In recent years, a collection of Wayburn's radio and noncommercial scripts has emerged at the University of Southern California.

The Billy Rose Theater Collection, New York Public Library for the Performing Arts, has been my primary source of printed material. Its clipping files, photographs (especially the White Studio key sheets), personal scrapbooks, and the four series of Robinson Locke Collection files and volumes have been of enormous assistance in my research. The Dance Collection, New York Public Library for the Performing Arts, has been another major source. Its collection of rare dance manuals, many donated by Lincoln Kirstein, has been invaluable. I am deeply grateful to the former curators Paul Myers and Genevieve Oswald, their successors Bob Taylor and Madeleine Nichols, and the staff of both collections for their kindness and help.

The two music collections of the New York Public Library for the Performing Arts—the Rogers and Hammerstein Archives of Recorded Sound and the Music Division—provided me with copies or transcriptions of much of the music that Wayburn wrote or used in his shows. Additional sources were found in other New York Public Library divisions: the Art and Architecture Division, the Newspaper Collection, U.S. Patent Office publications, the Rare Book and Manuscript Division's Sol Bloom Collection and Dr. Frank P. O'Brien Collection of dime novels (in which I was able to locate unexpected material on Colonel T. H. Monstery), and the Schomburg Center for Research in Black Culture.

Material was also found at the Theater and Music Collection, Museum of the City of New York; the Joseph Urban Papers, Rare Books and Manuscripts, Columbia University Library; the Edgar B. Wisely Collection of Recorded Sound, Brooklyn College, City University of New York; and the Information Service of the American Society of Composers, Authors, and Publishers.

Published and manuscript music was also located at the John Hay Library, Brown University, and the Music Division, Library of Congress. To John H. Stanley of the former institution and the staff of the latter, I am extremely grateful. I should also like to thank John Wayne of the U.S. Copyright Office for his kind assistance.

Many libraries in the Chicago and Denver areas were of great assistance in locating information on Wayburn's early years and on his teachers at the Hart Conway School of Acting. Among these were the Denver Public Library (Western History Division); University of Denver (University Archives); State Historical Society of Colorado (Chatauqua Collection); Chicago Historical Society (Divisions of Architecture and the Performing Arts); and the Newberry Library.

Material on François Delsarte was located at two university libraries. The Manuscript Collection of Louisiana State University houses Steele MacKaye's lectures on Delsarte. The MacKaye family papers, at the Baker Library, Dartmouth College, include these lectures as well as a manuscript notebook in the handwriting of Ida Simpson-Serven, Wayburn's teacher. I am very grateful to the staffs of these institutions for help in locating material and permission to copy the Simpson-Serven manuscript.

Additional material was found in the following collections: the Free Library of Philadelphia (Theater Collection and the Keefer Collection of Pre-1900 Music); the Margaret Herrick Library, Academy of Motion Picture Arts and Sciences; and the William Seymour Collection and Triangle Club Archives, Princeton University. I should also like to thank the archivist of Samuel Goldwyn Productions for her assistance in the vain attempt to locate prints of Wayburn's films.

For help in arranging interviews with former Wayburn dancers, I am grateful to the late Doris Vinton and Mrs. Dee of the New York and Los Angeles chapters of the Ziegfeld Club. I am also indebted to Fred Astaire, Florence O'Denishawn, Edward Claudius Weyburn, Jr., Chester Hale, and the members of the Ziegfeld Club for allowing me to interview them.

This book is dedicated with gratitude and affection to Lacy McDearmon, who gave me the copy of Wayburn's book, *The Art of Stage Dancing*, that started it all, and to my fellow dance students in the Department of Performance Studies, New York University.

—B.S.
New York City
April 1996

NED WAYBURN AND THE DANCE ROUTINE

Ned Wayburn was born Edward Claudius Weyburn in Pittsburgh, Pennsylvania, on 30 March 1874. His professional name, a misspelling of his original surname, was adopted after 1896, when he began to work in vaudeville. Both Wayburn's father, Elbert Delos, and his paternal grandfather, Chauncy, were inventors and manufacturers of industrial machinery. Chauncy Weyburn was known as an innovator in adapting the newly-invented sewing machine to industrial work, especially in the manufacture of leather goods. His son, Elbert Delos Weyburn, held more than one hundred patents for knitting and sewing machines, cutting machines for knit goods and burlap, vamp shapers (for shoe manufacturing), flexible groomers (for horses) and burglar alarms.[1]

As a child, Wayburn lived briefly in Atlanta, Georgia, but spent his adolescence in Chicago. He had some formal training as a pianist in both Atlanta and Chicago, but it is not known with whom he studied.[2] He and his brother Frank were expected to become engineers and inventors, and both studied mathematics and mechanical drawing at the Chicago Training School.[3] Wayburn worked as a draftsman on the Columbian Exposition of 1893, although which architectural firm employed him is unclear. His training as a pianist and as an architectural draftsman were to prove useful to him in his career.

Part of the Wayburn legend, at least as propagated by the choreographer in later life, was that he spent much of his adolescence running away from home to go onstage. He claimed to have worked as a call boy in Chicago for the Bijou Opera Company, the Chicago Museum, and the Olympia Theater, and to have been the "Rossiter" in the Hurricane Dutch and Irish Team of Johnson and Rossiter at Middleton's West Side Museum in the same city.[4] He may also have been a member of the team of Hafford and Rossiter Character Change Comedians that played at Chicago's Lyceum Theater in the week beginning 6 January 1893.[5] What is certain, however, is that while working in the family business, the Weyburn Machinery Company, he served as a supernumerary and as an usher at the Chicago Grand Opera House. Later, he worked in the same theater as chief usher and box office manager.[6] Finally, at the age of 21, he left the world of manufacturing and took a job as an accompanist and teacher at the Hart Conway School of Acting.

This institution, also known as the Chicago School of Elocution and the Conway Conservatory of Dramatic Art, offered classes in acting, dance, fencing, gymnastics, and physical culture, as well as presenting student recitals, amateur theatricals, and minstrel shows. Conway, a noted English-born character actor, has been described as "a member of the original Fifth Avenue Theater Company...especially selected by Edwin Booth for his splendid performances of the very difficult role of the 'Fool' in *King Lear....* [H]is 'Valreas' in the *Frou Frou* of [Helena] Modjeska is rightly remembered."[7] Mrs. Conway (Alice Brooks), who taught "rehearsal and stage training," had also been a member of the Modjeska company. It is not known whether Wayburn actually studied acting, but he did work with Conway as an assistant production stage manager for his semiannual school recitals and charity performances.[8] In 1897, after Wayburn had left the school, the Conways and their staff became affiliated with the Chicago Musical College, forming the nucleus of its School of Acting.[9] This conservatory was directed by its founder, Dr. Florenz Ziegfeld, Sr., the father of producers Florenz, Jr. and William Ziegfeld, with whom Wayburn worked frequently later in his career.

During Wayburn's tenure at the Conway School, the faculty included three teachers who, in various ways, fostered his growing interest in directing movement onstage. These were Professor C. H. Jacobsen, who taught "classic and fancy dancing"; Colonel T. H. Monstery, who taught "fencing and military drills"; and Mrs. Ida Simpson-Serven, who lectured on "voice and physical culture."[10]

Jacobsen, who began teaching at the Chicago Musical College before its affiliation with the Conway School, had been in the Chicago area since 1894. Little is known about his early life and dance training, although it is likely that he was the Karl Heinrich Jacobsen who entered the United States from Denmark in 1887 listed as a fiddler—the category under which many Danish dancing masters of the period emigrated.[11]

The terms "classic" and "fancy" dancing seem to have been used by Jacobsen to distinguish interpretive or neo-Greek dance from ballet, although there is not enough evidence to determine just what these terms meant to him. Neither category of dance was offered to men, but Wayburn, as a general assistant and pianist, may have accompanied or observed Jacobsen's classes. Both interpretive and balletic styles appeared in Wayburn's later choreography.

Colonel Thomas Hoyer Monstery, also of Danish descent, was a physical culturist as well as the author of the Beadle and Adams series of "dime and half-dime" novels for boys on such subjects as boxing, circuses, and war.[12] Born in Baltimore in 1824, he emigrated to Europe to serve in the Danish navy, studying fencing and swimming at the Royal Military College, Copenhagen. He then entered the Central Institute for Physical Culture, Stockholm, from which he graduated in the first class trained exclusively in the influential Per Henrik Ling system of gymnastics. This system, frequently called "educational gymnastics" in England and America, defined a progression of exercises that became popular in the United States during the 1890s, when the Boston, Philadelphia, and Cleveland school systems adopted the system.

Monstery studied fencing, gymnastics, and boxing in England, France, Spain, Italy, and Russia before returning to the United States in 1846. For the next twenty years, he taught fencing in Baltimore, Philadelphia, Cuba, Nicaragua, Honduras, El Salvador, Mexico, and the West Indies. He earned the title of colonel as instructor-at-arms in the Honduran army, and became known as "El Rubio Bravo," the Blond Mercenary or Assassin, the pen name that he adopted as a novelist. From 1861 to 1880 Monstery taught fencing and ran gymnasiums in San Francisco and New York. In 1880, he moved to Chicago, where he remained until his death. He taught at the Conway School and at a private studio from 1893 to 1897.

Two aspects of Monstery's training almost certainly had a special impact on Wayburn. The first was the Ling system, which he adopted, almost in its entirety, into the "stretching and limbering" exercises of the foundation course that was required of all students at the Wayburn studio.[13] In all probability, Wayburn was also influenced by the military drills that he studied with Monstery. Drill patterns appeared in many of Wayburn's numbers for precision dancers, especially during the World War I years, when patriotic numbers were popular.

The Conway School teacher who had the greatest influence on Wayburn was undoubtedly Ida Simpson-Serven, who taught the more theoretical side of physical culture—the aesthetic gymnastics of François Delsarte. Delsarte's concepts of meaningful gesture and breath control had an enormous impact on American dance, especially on the early pioneers of modern dance. Through Simpson-Serven, Wayburn was influenced by Delsarte methods as much as the modern dancers who viewed him as a symbol of meaningless Broadway entertainment.

Students in Wayburn's "foundation course" performing sit-ups and rollovers at his New York studio, ca. 1923. Promotional photograph, Billy Rose Theater Collection, New York Public Library for the Performing Arts.

Simpson-Serven had been an associate of director-playwright Steele MacKaye, himself a student of Delsarte, before moving to Denver in 1884.[14] MacKaye's letter granting her permission to use his name in advertising refers to "Mr. Serven's improved health" as resulting from this move.[15] Although it is not known whether the Winfield S. Serven mentioned in the letter was her father, husband, brother, or son, it can be assumed that her move to the West was precipitated by the tubercular condition of a close relative.

Once in Denver, she joined the faculty of O.B. Howell's Conservatory of Music. The 1888 Denver city directory listed her as a teacher of elocution at the University of Denver; the 1890 directory described her as the principal of the Denver Conservatory of the Arts. Between 1886 and 1889, she also performed at the Chautauqua Lyceum in the Denver area.[16]

Why Simpson-Serven moved to Chicago is unknown, although MacKaye's presence in the city beginning in 1893 was probably an inducement. She did not join the staff of the Chicago Musical College with the other faculty members of the Conway School, and was not listed in the Chicago city directory after 1896.

While little is known about Simpson-Serven's life, there is a great deal of information about her theories and teaching methods, since an extensive notebook of hers has been preserved in the MacKaye Family Papers at Dartmouth College.[17] This notebook, entitled "Harmonic Gymnastics," included a complete curriculum of vocal and physical culture and a table explaining the differences between her theories and those of the better-known American Delsartists, Genevieve Stebbins and Anna Morgan.

Wayburn almost certainly learned the aesthetic theories of physical cultural from Simpson-Serven. These included Delsartean ideas about the meaning of gestures and their ability to communicate emotion. The Delsarte principles that Wayburn adhered to most closely in his choreography were the laws of inflection, velocity, attitude, precision, and opposition.

By inflection, Delsarte meant that affirmative gestures tend to be perpendicular, negative gestures horizontal, and suspended gestures oblique. Wayburn made frequent use of oblique angles in his choreography—in the relation of the body to the proscenium and stage floor, the working leg to the supporting leg, and among the dancers in a line formation. Such angles occurred most commonly on the final beats of a bar, the cadence beat on which suspended notes and chords are typically placed. Attitude involved a similar series of contrasts: gestures representing positive emotions tend to rise, while those representing negative ones tend to fall. Wayburn's reliance on this law can be seen in the poses he frequently used to translate the lyrics of a song into movement, especially during the finale bars of the introduction to a song or in the transition measures between verse and refrain.

The complimentary laws of velocity and precision influenced Wayburn's choreography for groups performing the same movement in unison. The first stated that velocity is in proportion to "the mass moved and the force moving." Wayburn followed this law in "aural" dances, especially tap work, where the speed and density of sound were vitally important. In practical terms, it meant that the number of separate taps that could be heard by an audience was proportional to the number of performers executing them. Delsarte's law of precision stated that efficient force demands exactitude of movement and gesture—a definition of articulate tapping.

The law of opposition, which concerned the natural movement of the body, affected Wayburn's vocabulary of steps for "A-dancers," or show girls, especially what became known as the "Ziegfeld Walk." Rejecting the conventional opposition of arm and leg associated with fashion mannequins, he opted instead for a walk based on a spiral between the shoulders and pelvis. In the "Ziegfeld Walk," a show girl descending a staircase on the right side of the stage would balance her left shoulder with her right hip. Although Wayburn's choreography for show girls will be discussed in detail in a later chapter, it is important to mention here that the mannequin walk was a collaboration with the designer Joseph Urban. The staircase that Urban made a fixture of Wayburn's show girl processionals had steep risers. Wayburn was thus forced to create a special walk that would enable the dancers to negotiate the stairs without falling. Hence, the "Ziegfeld Walk," which was performed at an oblique angle to the audience and at the edge of the stair.

Wayburn taught Delsarte-derived tableaux and poses in his dance studios as part of "interpretive dancing," which was considered an important specialty of his studio. The ability to express emotion through the face, hands, and torso was considered necessary for all chorus performers and soloists. To instill expressiveness, Wayburn taught "descriptive" and "elliptic" pantomime, which was the name of an exercise described by Simpson-Serven in "Harmonic Gymnastics."[18] He spoke of his use of Delsarte's theories in many interviews. In 1916, a reporter for the *New York Tribune* wrote that "Mr. Wayburn is the only professor who regards the training of chorus girls strictly as a science. Mr. Wayburn drills his pupils in accordance with the doctrines first made known to a backward generation by one Delsarte...celebrated author of Mr. Wayburn's textbook and Bible, 'Sur l'Art de la Pantomime.'" He then quoted the choreographer as saying:

> I have merely put a theory into practice and arranged a definite routine for each day during the training period. I try to teach that all is not perspiration and no sense. For instance, by various positions of the hand clasp, the emotions of prayer, supplication, resignation or despair can be indicated. By constant repetition, I can compel the chorus to memorize these attitudes in regular sequence, and the numbers that I originate for songs are merely re-arrangements of the attitudes designed to tell the story in pantomime.[19]

Other important influences on Wayburn's choreography cannot be identified with specific individuals. These include ballet spectacles, minstrel shows, popular dances, and drills. All had a major impact on Wayburn's manipulation of groups, his recognition of symmetry as a choreographic theme, and his codification and handling of the routine format.

From Colonel Monstery or possibly an earlier grade or high school teacher, Wayburn learned the physical culture of military drills. These drills were ordered configurations for large groups of people, arranged in pairs, and moving in symmetrical paths. Many drill elements appeared in Wayburn's work. One was the emphasis on ordered steps, a vital element in drills; another was the use of symmetry, which was especially important in his collaborations with Urban.

In creating and codifying the routine format, Wayburn also drew on drill elements. In *The Art of Stage Dancing* he described the routine as follows:

> The average Routine consists of ten steps, one to bring you onto the stage, which is called a traveling step; eight steps to the dance proper, usually set to about 64 bars of music or the length of two choruses [i.e. refrains] of a popular song; and an exit step, which is a special step designed to form a climax to the dance and provoke the applause as you go off the stage....Routines are arranged so that they will provoke applause. Maybe the fourth or the eighth step will be climactic steps...to make the climax in the dance.[20]

The military drill was also based on this format. The participants marched onto the field, performed maneuvers, and then exited as a group. In such drills, the fourth and eighth maneuvers were designed to "provoke applause," as in Wayburn's routines. Wayburn even adopted some of the most effective poses associated with such maneuvers, such as ending a sequence facing front. This device was so deeply ingrained in Wayburn's work that the eight-direction chart—or "compass"—that he used in teaching listed front as the concluding direction of a movement.

Ballet spectacles were another source of influence on Wayburn. It is not known which spectacles he may have seen, but most of those produced in the United States in the 1880s and 1890s were revivals of works created in the post-Civil War period for imported French or Italian ballerinas. A key feature of these spectacles was their strictly hierarchical form, heightened by the gap in training and technique between the European soloists and the Americans in the pick-up corps de ballet. A similar, equally strict hierarchy prevailed in Wayburn's work, where the dancers were divided by technical expertise as well as physical type.

The variation was another key feature of such spectacles, and almost certainly an influence on Wayburn's formulation of the routine. Each routine, for instance, included traveling steps that could be repeated to create a showstopping effect. Even the repositioning typical of ballet variations—when the dancer walks upstage in preparation for a new sequence—had an equivalent in Wayburn's work. In many of his tap routines, for instance, the dancer moved upstage in a time step before launching into a diagonal cross.

The symmetry exhibited in military drills and in ballet corps work was also typical of minstrel shows, where an even number of performers was divided into two sections by a soloist. Wayburn was fascinated by minstrel shows as a child and recreated them frequently in his later work.[21] In some shows, he used minstrel-style makeup and costume: examples of this can be found in *Ned Wayburn's Minstrel Misses* (1903) and the 1922 edition of the *Ziegfeld Follies*. Other devices that he

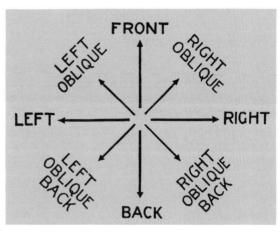

The eight directions of Wayburn's "compass."
Ned Wayburn, The Art of Stage Dancing *(1925), p. 45.*

adopted from minstrel shows included the parade, which appeared in almost every dance with more than twelve performers, and the shadow-graph or silhouette effect, which he used in *The Pearl and the Pumpkin* (1905), the *Ziegfeld Follies of 1923*, and many other shows.

Although movement by units of two or four performers to a regulated beat was a feature of military drills, ballet spectacles, and minstrel shows, it was also a fundamental element of the social dances popular during Wayburn's adolescence. Like many middle and upper-class young men of the period, Wayburn was thoroughly familiar with the cotillion.[22] Indeed, being six feet tall, musical, and the possessor of a booming voice, he had the attributes desirable in a cotillion leader, and served as such at dances given at the Great Northern Hotel, Chicago, which was owned by the father of his first wife, Agnes Saye. The position of leader required more than simply announcing the dance in the manner of a square dance caller: the leader had to "know precisely at what numerical beat in the music to begin and end the movement, the order of movements, and the ideal shape of the unfolding dance."[23] The job was excellent training for a future dance director.

The cotillion was not a spontaneous social dance. Each individual set of movements (called "figures") was taught by the leader, who had either invented them—which was unlikely, but possible in Wayburn's case—or studied them from published instructions. There were any number of books and pamphlets that a leader might consult to discover the timing and pathways of these figures. By the end of the nineteenth century, the eighty-three figures listed in Henri Cellarius's *Drawing Room Dances* (1847), which is considered the original cotillion manual, had grown to more than 250, most of which were performed throughout the country.[24] Figures created by dance masters for theme parties and balls were pub-lished in dance periodicals and the social pages of general interest magazines and newspapers, so that a figure invented in St. Louis or Buffalo might be performed in Chicago within a month.

Some of the most popular figures were task dances, in which a step or combination of steps had to be repeated until all the dancers were on the floor. Other figures had to do with the distribution of favors. The ones that seem to have influenced Wayburn the most involved the creation of shapes on the stage floor—shapes that remained invisible until all the dancers were in place. Certain cotillion-derived figures appear often in Wayburn's choreography, including the V, C, and W shapes, the serpentine coil, and the bisected circle.

Another cotillion figure that Wayburn adapted was the march. Marches typically inaugurated a ball or party. At a prearranged signal given by the leader, each man chose a partner and, with her, joined the line forming in the center of the room. As this could take time, the first march figure was always performed in a straight line, with changes in direction taking place at each end of the room: "one or two turns around the room," noted the author of an 1881 manual, "should be sufficient to enable all the couples who wish to participate to fall in line."[25] Three or four march figures would then be performed.

March figures followed one of two basic paths, although there were hundreds of variations. The first was a bisected circle, which could be formed with couples, pairs that separated, or an arbor of dancers. The other basic path followed the walls of the room and then formed either a serpentine spiral that coiled into the center of the room or a spine that reached from the center of the room to the sides. A popular variation of the latter was used to form the American flag: here, the spine moved to one side, while the dancers placed themselves on the other to make "stripes."[26]

Aesthetic and fancy drills were yet another late nineteenth-century social pastime that left a mark on Wayburn's choreography. Unlike the military version taught by Monstery, these drills were staged performances featuring tableaux and movements along prescribed paths. They were staged for participants of different ages and were usually sponsored by a social or educational organization. Drills, like cotillion figures, could be learned from instructional manuals; since drills required costumes (rather than social dress), many of these manuals were published by pattern companies and fashion magazines.

Aesthetic drills, which were performed in Grecian draperies, typically involved tableaux staged for an uneven number of female dancers. Scarves or garlands of real or artificial flowers were frequently used as props.[27] Considered a part of the American Delsarte movement, these drills were sometimes set to music or accompanied by the recitation of literary texts.[28]

Fancy drills, by contrast, could be performed by men as well as women in groups ranging in size from sixteen to 100. Staged for school and private entertainments, these drills were created around a theme that

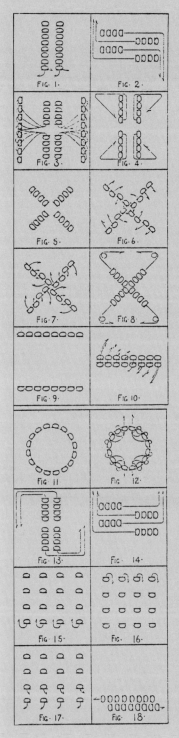

MARCH FOR SIXTEEN.

Enter, eight from the right and eight from the left, and march down the centre of stage or hall, as indicated in fig. 1.

When well down, first couple wheel to right, second to left, third to right, fourth to left, etc., march half way up on the sides of stage, and wheel so as to march across stage as indicated in fig. 2.

One division march up and the other march down stage, and go to centre to march toward each other and to the sides, as in fig. 3.

When in lines at sides of stage give signal by clapping hands (castanets may be used if preferred), and the two lines forward and stop when within about four feet of each other, and march as indicated by lines in fig. 4, forming star, fig. 5.

Sig. : all face as in fig. 6, and march once around as indicated by lines in fig. 6.

Each of the four arms of star wheel as indicated in fig. 7, which will bring centres to outside and outsides to centre. March once around as in fig. 6.

Sig. : all face as in fig. 8, and march as indicated, and form lines at back and front, facing, fig. 9.

Sig. : the two lines forward until they meet.

Sig. : wheel as indicated in fig. 10.

At finish of wheel all join hands and form circle, fig. 11.

Sig. : all let go of hands and about face quickly. Each kneel on right knee and extend both hands well forward and upward, all looking upward. Make short pause in this position.

Sig. : all rise and march as indicated by lines in fig. 12, which will bring all in position, as indicated in fig. 13.

March as indicated by lines in fig. 13, half the length of stage or hall, and cross, as in fig. 14.

March as indicated in fig. 14, and come down stage, four in line, hands joined and and extended the full length of arms.

Each file turn to right when down, and countermarch as indicated in fig. 15. The hands of those marching down should be kept joined until separated by the countermarch.

When well up the leader of each file turn again to right and lead a second countermarch, as in fig. 16, which will bring all in position, as in fig. 17.

Wheel to right and left, as indicated in fig. 17 (first line to right, second to left, etc.), and march up stage and come down eight in line. When well down Sig., front line kneel on right knees and extend right hands well to the front and upward, the left hands to the side and a little to the rear, joining them with left hands of those immediately behind, who should stand with weight on left foot, leaning a little forward, with right hands over heads, wrists curved. Those in front line looking up, those in rear line looking down. Make short pause in this position.

Sig. : front line rise and left face, rear line right face, and all march off single file.

Instructions for a march for sixteen performers. The Director, *Feb. 1898, p. 106.*

was echoed in the costumes and the props. Flowers and butterflies were favorite motifs, although foreign and topical ones were also popular. Typical of the latter were the Japanese fan drills that coincided with the height of the chinoiserie movement in decor and furniture design. Flag drills were also popular. "The Triple Flag Drill," created in 1898 during the Spanish-American War, made symbolic use of the Cuban, Spanish, and American flags, which were carried by groups representing the warring countries.[29] Wayburn used both fan and flag drills in the scene "In Old Japan" in *The Daisy Dancers* (1906).

A third type of fancy drill was really a cotillion performed by all-female couples. Here, the dancers manipulated accessories such as scarves or ribbons into braided or woven shapes. These drills were related to task dance figures, which also used these props and, like them, influenced Wayburn's later choreography.

Wayburn left the Conway School in 1896 with a letter of recommendation from Conway to Colonel John Hopkins of the State Street (later Hopkins) Theater, Chicago. The letter and an audition led to an engagement on the Keith circuit of vaudeville theaters as a blackface "rag-time pianist and monologuist."[30] Billed as "the man who invented rag-time," Wayburn built his act on the syncopating of familiar classical music pieces, such as Mendelssohn's "Wedding March" from the overture of *A Midsummer Night's Dream*. On reaching New York, he auditioned for the popular "coon-shouter" May Irwin and received a part as "Gregory, the rag-time Butler" in her new show, *The Swell Miss Fitzwell* (1897).[31] For this show, he not only appeared onstage as a musician but also served as assistant stage manager. In addition, he created lighting effects for the solo performed by his wife of the time, Agnes Saye.

After touring with the show, Wayburn was hired to perform in, write the music for, and stage *By the Sad Sea Waves* (1899). This show gave Wayburn his first experience with a professional chorus line. The line included a young San Franciscan named Kitty Hayes, who, as Gertrude Hoffmann, would become an important dance director and the star of two of his later shows. Their second show together, George Ade's *The Night of the Fourth* (1901), was conducted by "Baron" Max Hoffmann, who subsequently married Hayes and became Wayburn's favorite arranger and musical director.

Wayburn's emergence as a stage director followed quickly on his successful work for *The Night of the Fourth*. By the 1901-1902 season, he had settled into a schedule of staging a minimum of ten shows a year. By 1904, he was creating feature vaudeville acts for the producer-theater management teams of Oscar and William Hammerstein, and Marc Klaw and A. L. Erlanger. For Klaw and Erlanger, he also managed the New York Theater with designer F. Richard Anderson (then his brother-in-law) and directed a free dance school with arranger Fred Solomon.[32]

During this first decade of his career, Wayburn also worked on pantomimes and spectacle shows produced in New York and Chicago. For many of these undertakings, he received only partial staging credit, sharing the title of director with Herbert Gresham and choreographic responsibilities with the ballet master Ernest d'Auban.[33]

Between 1906 and 1913 Wayburn staged a wide variety of shows in New York and Chicago, while operating his own management firm, the Headline Vaudeville Production Company. During this period, he staged feature acts for his own firm, musical comedies for Lew Fields in New York and William Ziegfeld and Mortimer H. Singer in Chicago, and began a collaboration with the Shubert Brothers. For the Shuberts, he produced many musical comedies, operettas, and revues, including *Mlle. Mischief* (1908), two Hoffmann vehicles, *The Mimic World* (1908) and *Broadway to Paris* (1912), and the first two editions of the Shuberts' *Passing Show*, those of 1912 and 1913. He also produced a backstage musical vaudeville act, designed as a vehicle for himself. Unfortunately, no scripts for this feature act, called "The Producer," have survived.

Wayburn left New York in 1913 to stage an act called "Escalade" for the London Hippodrome, managed by Albert de Courville. This highly successful act was a reproduction of Wayburn's Act I finale for the 1913 *Passing Show* (where it was called "The Capitol Steps"), and Wayburn and de Courville vied with several London managers to be the first to produce the number in England. While in London, Wayburn staged revues for the Palladium and the Middlesex Music Halls as well. Returning to New York at the European outbreak of World War I, Wayburn leased the renovated Century Theater and presented his own *Town Topics* revue (1915).

In the spring of 1915, he accepted an exclusive engagement with Florenz Ziegfeld, Jr. as producing director. There is no evidence that Wayburn had worked with him before, despite his connection with his brother William in Chicago. In this first period of collaboration, Wayburn staged four editions of the *Ziegfeld Midnight Frolics* (1915-1919) and four of the *Ziegfeld Follies* (1916-1919), along with the Act II finale of *The Century Girl* (1916) and all of *Miss 1917*, these two shows being coproduced with Charles B. Dillingham.

Between 1919, when he quarreled with Ziegfeld, and 1922, when they worked together again on the *Follies*, Wayburn concentrated on the codification of his dance technique. This resulted in the textbook, *The Art of Stage Dancing*, published by his studio in six editions between 1923 and 1936. During these years, he also staged *The Ed Wynn Carnival* (1920) and *Two Little Girls in Blue* (1921) for Erlanger and *The Poor Little Ritz Girl* (1920) for Lew Fields. At the same time, he experimented with a new theatrical genre—the Prolog. A form of live performance, designed to introduce a feature film and tour with it, Prologs made their appearance just after the war and were produced on contract from film studios. Like Wayburn, many choreographers took up the new genre—John Murray Anderson, Maria Gambarelli, and Chester Hale in New York; Boris Petroff and Jack Partington in Chicago; and Fanchon and Marco in Los Angeles. Wayburn created Prologs for four of the era's biggest movie chains: MGM, including its flagship Capitol Theater in New York (for which he produced the *Demi-Tasse Revues* and *Ned Wayburn's Song Scenes*); the Paramount-Publix Corporation; the combined Keith, Albee, and Orpheum chains; and Famous Player-Laskey Films (with Ben Ali Haggin as codirector)—all between 1919 and 1933.[34]

Wayburn did his last editions of the *Follies* in 1922 and 1923. A scene

Cartoon by W. C. Fields, 1920. The "little boys" are Charles B. Dillingham ("C.B.D."), A. L. Erlanger ("A.L.E."), Florenz Ziegfeld, Jr. ("F.Z."), and Edward Franklyn Albee ("E.A."). Ned Wayburn Scrapbook 21,067, Billy Rose Theater Collection, New York Public Library for the Performing Arts.

from the second show was restaged for the film *The Great White Way* (Cosmopolitan Pictures, 1924), with Wayburn himself appearing as the dance director who overworks a chorus girl (Anita Stewart) until she faints and tumbles down a flight of stairs. Stewart's stunt double was Evelyn Law, who performed a Wayburn routine in the only other film with which he is believed to have been involved—*Potash and Perlmutter* (Samuel Goldwyn Productions, 1923). Unfortunately, both films appear to be lost.

Wayburn staged no complete shows that reached Broadway between 1923 and 1930. There are many possible explanations for this. After twenty-five years of nonstop work, he may simply have decided to slow down. However, it is also possible that his fondness for large chorus numbers—at a time when "little shows" were becoming increasingly popular—worked against him. According to Fred Astaire, who starred in Wayburn's final Broadway show, *Smiles* (1930), the musical was actually a "doctoring job" done as a favor for Ziegfeld.[35] Nevertheless, throughout the period, Wayburn continued to stage many new shows—school recitals, Prologs, college club performances, and a number of industrial shows. A list of Wayburn's most important shows appears in the chronology at the end of this book.

Wayburn's retirement from Broadway did not end his theatrical career. His studios remained going concerns, although the curriculum now shifted from straight dance training to a combination of dance, radio and film acting, and singing. Before his death in September 1942, Wayburn became interested in television production and performance. He had taught television techniques at his New York studio for more than two years, and was scheduled to appear as host of *The Search for Beauty* (NBC-Blue Channel) on the afternoon of 7 December 1941. That day, Japanese bombs fell on Pearl Harbor, and all entertainment broadcasting was canceled. Wayburn never made his TV debut.

Dance Idioms and Performance Hierarchies

The choreographic examples discussed in the following chapters represent the three major genres that Wayburn explored throughout his career—feature acts, individual specialty acts, and chorus acts. All relied on the technical idioms or vocabularies that Wayburn employed in his work regardless of genre and revealed the spatial and performance hierarchies that were a trademark of his dance direction.

Wayburn based his choreography on six "techniques": musical comedy dance, tapping and stepping, acrobatic work, "modern Americanized ballet," toe specialties, and exhibition ballroom dancing. Each of these idioms could be used in chorus work or as the basis of an individual specialty act. If used in a specialty number, each could be treated in one of several "modes": "eccentric," "normal," "acrobatic," or "characterizational."

Musical comedy technique was the idiom that Wayburn employed in most of his chorus and specialty choreography. The term itself is somewhat misleading, for the technique was neither limited to musical comedies nor even chiefly employed in them. Wayburn described musical comedy technique in *The Art of Stage Dancing*:

> It is a cross between the ballet and...tap and step dancing. It combines pretty attitudes, poses, pirouettes and the several different types of kicking steps. Soft-shoe steps break into it here and there in unexpected ways and places, adding a pleasing variety to the menu. The tempo enhances and harmonizes the scene....The dance is full of happy surprise steps, perhaps, or unexpected climaxes and variations that arouse the interest as they quickly flash by.[1]

The vocabulary of Wayburn's musical comedy technique derived from soft-shoe dancing, ballet, and tap. The basic foot movements were the step (a single movement performed with the full foot touching the floor), the drag (pulling the full foot, toe, or heel along the floor toward the supporting foot), and the touch (used to shift weight and to emphasize a beat). Steps were angled to all eight directions of Wayburn's stage compass, but kicks to front right or front left predominated. The step turns used in this technique were frequently broken down into two, three, four, or even eight movements.

The difference between the "normal" and "eccentric" treatment of musical comedy steps was clearest in kicking steps. Dancers working in the standard mode would perform front, back, and side kicks to a height of no more than fifty degrees. Eccentric soloists, by contrast, kicked to 180 degrees, while also doing combinations of kicks, such as the hitch kick and the pendulum, in which the working leg would swing from back to front without shifting weight. Evelyn Law and Ann Pennington were among those known for their hitches—combination kicks that ended with the foot well above the ear. Law, in fact, was famous for her ability to hop across the stage while maintaining her "hitch."

Dances in musical comedy style sometimes included "characterizational" specialties for the chorus. These ranged from soldier and doll dances to hula shimmies. In these shimmies, which will be discussed in the chapter on individual specialty acts, the step patterns were virtually identical to those in standard musical comedy work, with the same emphasis on oblique angles and step turns.

Wayburn also employed musical comedy technique in numbers for small groups of precision dancers. His use of the idiom can be traced directly to the Original English Pony Ballet, an English precision troupe that made its New York debut in 1883 in *The Casino Girl*.[2] Consisting of eight short dancers trained at the John Tiller School in London, the chorus displayed the absolute precision of movement that Tiller had made the trademark of his choreography. Thus, even when performing in

Evelyn Law in the final movement of a hitch kick. She is wearing the costume for the "Rambler Rose" scene in the Ziegfeld Follies of 1922. *Ned Wayburn,* The Art of Stage Dancing *(1925), p. 114.*

"normal" musical comedy style, with kicks limited to fifty degrees, the Original English Pony Ballet danced with a unison that translated the steps into an eye-filling experience. The dancers frequently used accessories—hoops and sticks, flower bouquets and parasols—that extended their arm movements and accented the dance steps.[3]

Wayburn worked with the Original English Pony Ballet frequently between 1903 (*Mr. Bluebeard*) and 1913, when his Headline Vaudeville Company assumed the management of the troupe. He also staged precision dances in many shows and acts for similar types of small groups of short women. It is possible, in fact, that Wayburn's fascination with the precision style delayed the development of his other idioms.

Until the mid-1910s tapping and stepping was considered a solo or duo specialty. The technique, which Wayburn believed was derived from clog dancing, was used for vaudeville acts and individual solos interpolated or worked into shows.[4] The transition from an individual specialty to a chorus technique can be traced to the "soldier" numbers that appeared in revues during World War I. Like other dance directors, Wayburn recognized the advantage of integrating sound into the actual marching of the dancers, instead of adding it more conventionally through the percussion section of the orchestra.

This particular form of chorus work had a major drawback: although any number of performers could be accommodated onstage (thanks to the growing popularity of sets featuring platforms and staircases), only a limited number of dancers could tap before the sounds became muffled. This problem was never resolved in stage work; in Vitaphone and Movietone films, however, where the taps were added through sound editing, dance directors were able to employ large numbers of dancers, while maintaining the clarity of the sound.

The chief difference between musical comedy and tap steps was the presence in the latter of sound. The footwork was more articulated, and eventually Wayburn spelled out six different ways the shoe made contact with the floor. No fewer than four were taught at his studio in the first class in tap and stepping.[5] After learning the straight (flat foot), front, back, and heel taps, beginning dancers studied shoe-edge articulation, the time step, and the break—all in the first week of classes.[6]

The other major difference between musical comedy and tap work was the time it took to perform an individual step. In musical comedy work, kicks and step turns were used to enhance a routine. In tapping and stepping, by contrast, both were dead time, since they did not create any sound. Pivots, which Wayburn rejected in musical comedy work, were important in tap work as they were the only way to shift direction without making noise.[7]

Wayburn created a number of character type dances using tap technique. These included "drunk" and doll dances, and a specialty known as "Russian" or "Cossack" tap, which was popular in the mid-1920s. This specialty, associated with Ivan Bankoff and Ada May Weeks, was basically a *kazachok* or *tallone*—a Cossack folk dance performed in tap shoes.

Eccentric tap work, or "legomania," was popular from the mid-1910s until well into the 1930s. Legomania consisted of tap dancing with the high kicks and step turns of musical comedy technique. The style required great control and articulation since much of the tapping was performed with the supporting foot, while the working foot was hitched into the air.

Legomania was originally a form of acrobatic dancing and was taught at the Wayburn studios as a chorus technique. Later, when it became associated with tap work, Wayburn replaced it with other acrobatic movements. Among the acrobatic steps used by Wayburn in routines choreographed in the early 1920s were backbends, handstands, traveling handstands (or inside-outs), front-overs (a forward straight-leg flip), cartwheels, and various somersaults. Splits, performed to the front or side, were also a part of Wayburn's acrobatic technique.

Acrobatic dances of a character type were seldom staged by Wayburn for women. Typically emphasizing loss of balance or control, these dances included "drunk" acts and "boat deck" acts. In the latter, the male dancer would lurch and slide around the stage.

The third technique that Wayburn employed in his choreography was what he called "modern Americanized ballet." In 1923, he claimed to have "invented a method of teaching the ballet that eliminates the long and tedious training formerly considered necessary, and fits the pupil for a stage appearance in the briefest possible length of time."[8] This claim, which is typical of the promotional literature of the day, can be taken literally. A dancer could indeed learn enough ballet technique in a year of daily classes at the Wayburn studio to appear onstage. She studied it, however, with classically trained Europeans, not with Wayburn.[9] The teachers employed by his studio were for the most part exponents of Italian technique, and one can assume that they taught the basics of that style to their American students.[10]

The vocabulary of Wayburn's modern Americanized ballet was limited to a dozen categories of steps, all of which were performed pizzicato and terre à terre, quickly and sharply. The most frequently employed traveling steps were bourrées, performed opened or closed, turning or moving straight in any direction. Wayburn frequently used a combination step that he called "point step forward" that was really another form of bourrée. Various kinds of piqué turns were also used as a traveling step.

Wayburn often adapted elements from other idioms into his ballet choreography. His pivoting échappés, for instance, were a balletic version of the step turns that he frequently used in musical comedy work. He liked fouettés, which ended—as did some of his favorite drill maneuvers—in a pose facing directly front.

Wayburn tended to avoid character styles in ballet. He made extensive use, however, of both eccentric and acrobatic forms. The difference between these styles was based on the degree of displacement from standard ballet posi-

Virginia Bacon in an acrobatic ballet pose.
Ned Wayburn, The Art of Stage Dancing *(1925), p. 137.*

tions. In eccentric work, exaggerated stretches displaced the hip and pelvis; in acrobatic ballet, normal footwork might be performed in a deep backbend.

A fourth form of ballet that appeared in Wayburn's choreography beginning in the early 1910s was known as "toe tapping" or "trick ballet." For this technique, conventional pointe shoes were fitted with metal Haney plates, which created a tapping sound when the shoe made contact with the floor. Although the form was viewed by many as a "compromise" of the art of "serious" solo dancers such as Mazie King, Gladys Moore, and Bessie Clayton, trick ballet was essentially a group technique, designed for precision teams. The vocabulary was similar to that of Wayburn's modern Americanized ballet, but bourrées were eliminated. The most important steps were those that involved some form of rotation, since this provided the greatest amount of visual movement with the least amount of sound.

Toe tapping was popular, but never really successful as a group technique. Although audiences reveled in its physical difficulties, Wayburn and other choreographers found it inflexible. As in conventional tap work, the sound elements could not be properly controlled: a dancer could not change position or direction without making noise. Moreover, it is unlikely that many dancers could achieve full articulation given the nature of their shoes.

The last major idiom used by Wayburn was exhibition ballroom dancing. This consisted of theatricalized versions of popular social dances. During Wayburn's career, these dances were two-steps (including hesitations and the Castle Walk), one-steps (including glides, the Turkey Trot, and the Grizzly Bear), tangos, and maxixes. After 1919, the Black Bottom and the Charleston became popular. Finally, after 1924, one-steps and tangos returned to popularity.

The theatricalizing process was different for each dance form. Two-steps were altered by adding syncopated pauses; one-steps, tangos, and maxixes by exaggerating holds. The Turkey Trot and Grizzly Bear had dips, bends, and sways. As solo ballroom dances, the Black Bottom and the Charleston were easily theatricalized by the addition of a chorus to frame the dancing soloists.

Wayburn's choreography and stage direction rested upon a strict hierarchy of performers. This applied to all acts and to all musical numbers in which more than one performer appeared. The simplest hierarchy was created for feature acts in which only two kinds of performers participated—a soloist and a unison chorus. In many of these acts, the soloist was positioned in front of the massed chorus, either on the apron of the stage or in the center of a semicircle or a V-shaped configuration.

Beginning around 1910, the chorus itself became increasingly differentiated. Until then, the female chorus dancers in most musical comedies, revues, and pantomimes had been classified by height and the ability to perform on pointe. From a choreographic point of view, this reflected the

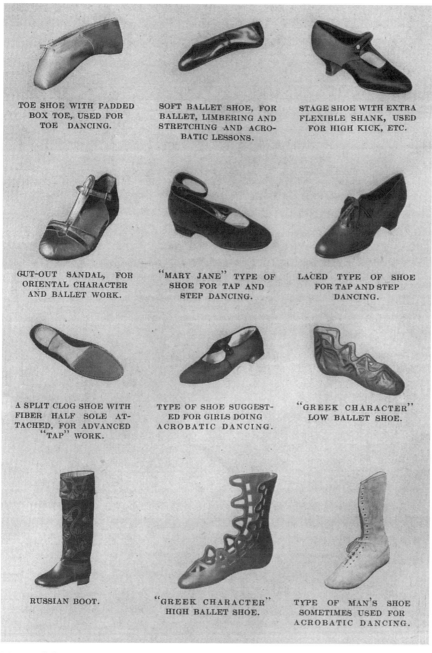

TOE SHOE WITH PADDED BOX TOE, USED FOR TOE DANCING.

SOFT BALLET SHOE, FOR BALLET, LIMBERING AND STRETCHING AND ACROBATIC LESSONS.

STAGE SHOE WITH EXTRA FLEXIBLE SHANK, USED FOR HIGH KICK, ETC.

CUT-OUT SANDAL, FOR ORIENTAL CHARACTER AND BALLET WORK.

"MARY JANE" TYPE OF SHOE FOR TAP AND STEP DANCING.

LACED TYPE OF SHOE FOR TAP AND STEP DANCING.

A SPLIT CLOG SHOE WITH FIBER HALF SOLE ATTACHED, FOR ADVANCED "TAP" WORK.

TYPE OF SHOE SUGGESTED FOR GIRLS DOING ACROBATIC DANCING.

"GREEK CHARACTER" LOW BALLET SHOE.

RUSSIAN BOOT.

"GREEK CHARACTER" HIGH BALLET SHOE.

TYPE OF MAN'S SHOE SOMETIMES USED FOR ACROBATIC DANCING.

Types of shoes recommended for use at the Ned Wayburn studio in the 1920s. Ned Wayburn, The Art of Stage Dancing *(1925), p. 266.*

division of tasks between the ballet master (responsible for "toe" dancing and specialties such as aerial dancing) and the dance director (who handled the general movement and the "Amazon" line). Height was the distinction used to establish gender: short women played females, and tall women played males.

After *The Mimic World* (1908) and *The Midnight Sons* (1909), Wayburn began to divide the female chorus into three to five groups based on height and to assign specific techniques to each class of dancers. The shortest women, known as "ponies," were taught tap work and modern Americanized ballet; the tallest, "A-dancers" or show girls, were trained to pose and move decoratively in processionals. The middle-sized groups, which could be split into two smaller ones, were the utility dancers who worked in the musical comedy technique. Wayburn adhered to this system of differentiation until the end of his stage career.

Wayburn's use of hierarchy—as a device establishing the primacy of the soloist and as a method of differentiating the chorus—was revealed with exceptional clarity in the shows he staged for Ziegfeld. Indeed, by the time he mounted the *Follies of 1922*, he could place an entire cast onstage, knowing that its rankings would be fully—and immediately—legible to the audience.

The piano player is more of a hero than a stage manager. The manager doesn't have to look at the show—the pianist does.[1]

Ned Wayburn made the transition from piano player to producing stage manager through his experiments with feature acts. From 1901 to 1909 he created over 120 of these short numbers, which averaged twenty-five minutes in length and were complete in themselves. Acts were generally divided into three, four, or five scenes and ranged in form from musical comedies and revues to melodramas. Musical acts emphasized precision choreography; all acts, whether musical or not, had elaborate design elements. Feature acts were staged in New York and reworked for subsequent vaudeville tours.

Wayburn's production of feature acts can be divided into two periods. The second began in 1906, with the founding of his Headline Vaudeville Production Company, which allowed him to maintain full artistic control over production. From 1901 to 1905, however, he created acts on commission from the managers of New York's summer roof theaters—the Paradise Garden Roof Theater, owned and run by Oscar and William Hammerstein, and Klaw and Erlanger's New York Theater Roof and Crystal Garden Theater.

Wayburn's early career was bound up with the history of New York's roof theaters, which, like the summer season, came into existence at the turn of the century. Since roof theaters were managed as cabarets, with food and alcoholic beverages served at tables, they died with Prohibition, which cut deeply into their business. As a revenue-producing device, the summer season was extremely successful. Audiences could spend two comfortable hours in a roof theater, while even a few minutes inside a stifling Broadway playhouse—this was the era before air conditioning—was unbearable. As *The Theatre Magazine* wrote in 1904:

> The roof garden, as a refuge from the higher temperatures of the streets and of ordinary homes, and as a means of diversion, has become a distinctive feature of summer life in New York [where] a certain altitude [can] afford more unfailing cooling breezes. Summer audiences care little for serious entertainment; the slightest mental effort makes them perspire and a respite from the dramatic will be granted by every manager alive to his own interests.[2]

Between 1901 and 1906, the Hammersteins' roof theater presented both vaudeville bills and full-evening musical comedies, although Wayburn created only feature acts for them. For Oscar Hammerstein, feature acts served to provide employment for his performers and business for his theater; it seems likely, however, that Klaw and Erlanger used them to audition individual specialty acts for their vaudeville production company and talent agency. It also seems probable that Wayburn himself was being auditioned at this time, since, in the three years between the announcement that he intended to open his own production company and the realization of the plan, Klaw and Erlanger gave him the management of their New York Theater and the directorship of their free School of Stage Dancing.

There were certain differences between the acts staged by Wayburn for the Hammersteins and those he created for Klaw and Erlanger. In general, the differences were based on the requirements concerning the hiring and employment of soloists. Acts created for the Hammersteins featured a single soloist, usually a female vocalist-comedienne at the beginning of her career. The soloists for whom Wayburn staged the two acts that opened the Paradise Garden seasons in 1901 and 1902, for example, were Eleanor Falk and Countess Olga von Hatzfeldt, both of whom went on to star in Oscar Hammerstein's *Parsafalia* (1904).

The acts that Wayburn choreographed for Klaw and Erlanger, on the other hand, employed both male and female soloists. *Ned Wayburn's Girls of 1904*, for example, had five soloists: vocalists Josephine Davis and Nellie V. Nichols, musician Luke Pulley, and the "coon-shouters"—or early blues singers—Emma Carus and Tascott.[3]

The design elements in these early acts were the most inexpensive and primitive of Wayburn's career. The scenery, by and large, consisted of painted wings and drops showing pastoral scenes. With one exception—a scene in *Ned Wayburn's Girls of 1904* where a "Waltz Clog" was danced on foot-high pedestals placed on three tiers of platforms—the movement in these acts was confined to the stage floor.

The costumes worn by the large choruses in Wayburn's early acts were derived from nineteenth-century spectacle shows. The dancers were dressed either in "Prince Charmings"—a "combination" consisting of a jacket, short trousers, and tights that was based on male attire of the Empire period—or in costumes designed to represent a particular period, place, or occupation.[4] In *The Sunny South* (1901), considered Wayburn's first feature act, the chorus wore Prince Charmings in the opening scene, short polka-dot cakewalk crinolines in the title number, and Japanese kimonos in the finale. Female soloists, on the other hand, appeared in contemporary dress—ankle-length gowns, long-sleeved bodices with a high neckline, and wide-brimmed hats.

No lighting effects are mentioned in reviews of Wayburn's early feature acts. Lighting, however, became a significant element once he assumed control of the production, budgeting, and management of his own acts. It is certainly possible that managers anxious to minimize costs kept him from building sophisticated lighting effects into the acts he did on commission.

Vaudeville tours for Wayburn's early commissioned acts were arranged by the roof theater managers, and the acts were performed chiefly in theaters belonging to the Keith and Proctor chains. In 1906, however, Wayburn decided to set up his own producing company and to offer acts independently to the vaudeville chains, without the intervention of Klaw and Erlanger or the Hammersteins. His organization, the Headline Vaudeville Production Company, eventually produced and managed over 100 touring feature acts, including *The Rain-dears* (1906), with the singer Neva Aymar; *The Side Show* (1908), with the exhibition ballroom dancer Harry Pilcer; *The Phantastic Phantoms* (1907), with the acrobats Hilarion and Rosalia Ceballos; and *The Daisy Dancers* (1906), which will be discussed in detail below.[5] The Headline company also produced nonmusical feature acts, most of which were melodramas based on sporting events. In *The Futurity Winner* (1906) and *The Star Bout* (1908), for example, the climax took place, respectively, at an onstage horse race and a boxing match.

The musical acts produced by Wayburn between 1906 and 1913 were structured like miniature revues. Each had five scenes linked together by a loose theme—weather in the case of *The Rain-dears*; the circus in *The Phantastic Phantoms* and *The Side Show*. Because the Headline company operated its own scenic, costume, and lighting studios, Wayburn could incorporate a theme into all the design elements of an act. *The Side Show*,

The Phantastic Phantoms *(1907). The top photograph shows an acrobatic pose; the lower one, an early Wayburn chair dance. Ned Wayburn unmounted clipping file, Robinson Locke Collection, Billy Rose Theater Collection, New York Public Library for the Performing Arts.*

for example, used mechanized pumps to inflate the costumes worn in one scene, while *The Phantastic Phantoms* toured with its own portable black box set, complete with trapeze rigging and a lighting system.[6] Both *The Rain-dears* and *The Daisy Dancers* traveled with gutter systems that permitted special effects to be created; in the latter, the system was used to shower the stage with daisies, while in the former, it produced a snow-storm.[7]

In these mini-revues the hierarchical relationship between the soloists and the chorus was less strictly observed than in Wayburn's commissioned acts. In the earlier productions, the soloist would perform on the apron of the stage in front of the chorus. In the later acts, however, the soloist frequently joined the chorus line and performed the same movements. The integration of soloists and specialty performers, always a major concern in Wayburn's work, was achieved in different ways in each production. In *The Rain-dears*, Neva Aymar was completely integrated into the line of dancers; in *The Phantastic Phantoms*, Hilarion and Rosalia Ceballos hovered above the chorus on trapezes; in the cabaret scene in *The Side Show*, Harry Pilcer performed a different ballroom dance with each member of the chorus.

The music used both in the commissioned acts and in the acts produced by Wayburn's own company consisted of ragtime syncopation arrangements of existing songs. Most of the songs were by Wayburn himself, his arrangers Max Hoffmann and Fred Solomon, or the team of William Jerome and Jean Schwartz. Wayburn also used songs by Bob Cole and J. Rosamond Johnson, Byrd Dougherty, Gus Edwards, Al Johns, Edward Madden (with Schwartz or Dorothy Jardon), Theodore F. Morse, and Harry von Tilzer. Between 1901 and 1913, all were involved in writing original ragtime and in "ragging the classics," the piano playing novelty that had been Wayburn's own vaudeville specialty.[8]

Certain elements were common to all of Wayburn's feature acts in this period, and his manipulation of them foreshadowed the work of his later career. The first and most important concerned the organization of the performers onstage; the second, his fascination with quick changes of costume, makeup, and scenery, especially changes that were visible to the audience.

In his treatment of stage space Wayburn began with basic solutions—the straight line and the semicircle, or arch. In the opening scene of *The Sunny South*, the twenty-four dancers (in Prince Charmings) were arranged in lines of six, "according to the color of their hair, just like cavalry horses."[9] Within each of the four sets, they were lined up by height.[10] At two points in the scene, the lines moved together to form a double row of deep semicircles, with the tallest dancers from each hair-color group grouped at the center of each "arch." A photograph of the scene shows another line-up by height: this time the shortest dancers were at stage left, and the tallest ones at stage right. This configuration was also used in the kimono scene, although, in this instance, the semicircles were shallower.

In the title scene—in which half the chorus was dressed in dark polka-dot crinolines, and half in white ones—the twenty-four dancers formed a rectangle of four rows of six, with the vertical lines alternating by dress color. The shape, with its alternating stripes of color, then stretched into a parallelogram, with two dancers remaining at downstage right and two others at upstage left.

In *The Three CH's (CHic, CHarm and CHaste)* (1902), Wayburn used four-sided shapes again, although this time he worked with eighteen dancers instead of twenty-four. A photograph of the Southern scene shows the chorus in a double parallelogram composed of two sets of nine dancers in three rows of three.[11] The upstage dancers met at stage center, forming a rough V-shape bisecting the parallelograms. Although Wayburn seems to have lost interest in rectangular shapes on flat stage floors after this show, he retained the V-outline, which became a trademark of his staging.

The opening "Jockey Club" scene in *The Three CH's* may well represent Wayburn's first real success in accommodating an organizational plan to a design motif. The choreography was simple: an entrance march performed by two lines of nine dancers, followed by a dance performed first in three rows of six, then in a double row of semicircles of ten and eight. The dancers, however, were costumed in jockey uniforms, each of which represented a New York stable. Bertie Herron, Girl Number Seventeen, for instance, wore the canary jacket and black sash of the A. Fetherston Stables.[12] The stables had been chosen with an eye to the color and pattern relationships that would be formed by the dancers as they moved through the various configurations. Wayburn was to employ design motifs often in his choreography, especially in his finales for the *Ziegfeld Follies*, where he masterfully assembled the differentiated choruses into a visually arresting stage picture involving the whole cast.

Wayburn favored the eighteen-woman chorus until the formation of the Headline Vaudeville Production Company in 1906. For reasons that may have involved finances or simply the knowledge that the more elaborate scenery that he hoped to use would occupy more space, Wayburn reduced the chorus to six or eight. Another factor in the shift to a smaller chorus may have been his renewed interest in the eight-woman Original English Pony Ballet.

Whatever the reason for the change, the smaller chorus required new staging effects. Wayburn could no longer rely on the impact of a march to open a scene, so he was forced to invent new ways of getting the chorus onstage. He found, too, that he could no longer use sheer numbers to create shapes on the stage, and that costumes or props were needed to produce connective lines between and among the dancers. In the prologue to *The Rain-dears*, for example, the eight-woman chorus danced with hoops and sticks, and in the final storm scene, manipulated oversized umbrellas.[13] In both scenes, the formation was a simple line across the stage. During the cabaret scene of *The Side Show*, the eight women were placed either on a diagonal (from upstage right to downstage center) or in a V shape (from downstage right and left, meeting at upstage center). These formations had two functions: they allowed the chorus to frame the solo dancer, and they enabled Wayburn to change and limit the amount of empty stage space. This second function was especially important in the cabaret scene because the ballroom dances of 1907-1909 employed very short steps. To fill the stage space Pilcer would have had to lengthen his stride to such an extent as to recast the choreography in an eccentric or acrobatic mode.[14]

Wayburn's ability to use both chorus sizes—eighteen to twenty-four and six to eight—played a large part in his growing reputation as a dance director who could handle any show. Another aspect of his work on feature acts that helped win him that reputation was his imaginative use of the quick change as a production element.

His first experiments in this realm involved makeup. In *Minstrel Misses* (1903), probably his only feature act conceived as a single scene, a chorus of sixteen women marched onstage wearing "the long coats of fantastic design and collar and high hats of a Minstrel parade."[15] Then, "in full view of the audience," the dancers made themselves up in blackface at tables set at the rear of the stage.[16] The sequence took only ninety seconds to perform, but it made the reputation of the act, which ran for eleven months on tour.[17]

Wayburn also used the same device in the "Dinjies" scene of his 1904 *Girls* act.[18] It is unclear whether the makeup transformed the dancers into "Dinges" (then, a slang term for African Americans) or exotic Middle Eastern "Djinnies."[19] The former is more likely, as the accompanying music for the scene was Theodore F. Morse's "Dixie" Overture.

Wayburn was interested in developing costumes that would permit quick changes in full view of the audience. He claimed to have patented a "new trick dress" allowing the dancer to make "five instantaneous changes on stage," although, in fact, no patent was granted for the invention.[20] *The Rain-dears*, for which the dress was ostensibly invented, did require five costume changes for each member of the cast, but it is not known whether the "trick dress" was actually used.[21] Wayburn also experimented with costumes that could be transformed onstage. In the circus scene of *The Side Show*, for example, half the chorus wore rubber suits that inflated until the dancers resembled Tweedledum and Tweedledee.[22]

With the increasing use of differentiated choruses by Wayburn and other choreographers, quick change costumes became less important since one chorus group could change while another was onstage. Instantaneous set changes remained essential to Wayburn, however, and he continued to explore scenic devices that could cut "dead" time. Although most of these experiments were made between *Town Topics* (1915) and the *Demi-Tasse* and *Song Scenes* revues (1920-1921), by 1906 he had already begun to require sets that could be changed quickly and easily.

Ned Wayburn's Minstrel Misses *(1902), showing the minstrel parade and various members of the cast in blackface. Bertie Herron Scrapbook, Robinson Locke Collection, Billy Rose Theater Collection, New York Public Library for the Performing Arts.*

His earliest experiments used the same simple systems. The drops for the final two scenes of *The Rain-dears* and the first two scenes of *The Daisy Dancers* were hung in such a way that, when they were raised, a new one was revealed. The fact that the sets were merely painted canvases was disguised to some extent in *The Rain-dears* by simulated snow and rainstorms, and in *The Daisy Dancers* by elaborate chorus entrances using moving set pieces, including a gypsy wagon drawn by a live donkey.

The elements of staging and design that so influenced Wayburn's later work can be seen in *The Daisy Dancers*. This act, which Wayburn later listed as one of his major accomplishments,[23] played for over eight months in New York and on tour. Variously billed as *Dancing Daisies* and *Daisyland*, it opened its pre-New York City tour at the Proctor Theater in Troy, New York, during the week beginning 21 May 1906. Two weeks later, it began a run at Proctor's 23rd Street Theater, New York City, where it played for eleven weeks. It later toured the Proctor chain of vaudeville theaters as far south as Baltimore and as far west as Cincinnati, before returning to the New York City area. The last booking for the act was a week in Trenton, New Jersey, beginning 6 November 1906, although the act continued to be listed on the Headline Vaudeville Production Company's letterhead until 1917.[24]

The scenery for the act was designed by A.M. Langstaff and painted by Ernest M. Gros of the Headline company studio. The costumes were designed and executed by Corene Uzell, who was also a member of the chorus. The music was arranged by Fred Solomon from songs by Bob Cole and J. Rosamond Johnson ("Mexico"), Gus Edwards ("Pocohontas"), William Jerome and Jean Schwartz ("My Little Lady of Japan" and "Daisyland"), and Edward Madden and Dorothy Jardon ("The Yankee Boy in Blue"). The program credit—"devised and staged by Ned Wayburn"—was used by Wayburn in all his later feature acts.

Dorothy Jardon, a popular monologuist, singer, and composer, starred in the act. The eight-woman chorus, at the time of the first performance, consisted of Mabel Bonner, Esther Boggs, Della Kessner, Julia Lamaedrid, Zadora Porter, Hazel Sanger, Cleo Sparling, and Corene Uzell—all trained at the free school that Wayburn and Fred Solomon directed for Klaw and Erlanger.

When *The Daisy Dancers* opened in Troy, the act contained four separate scenes—"In Old Mexico," "In Old Japan," "In Old Virginia," and "In Daisyland."[25] Each scene featured a song ("Mexico," "My Little Lady of Japan," "Pocohontas," and "Daisy," which was also known as "Daisyland") and had different costumes and scenery. The format for each segment was that of an extended routine, beginning with a song or monologue by Jardon that introduced the chorus dance.

Scene 1, "In Old Mexico," opened with a monologue and the song "Mexico," describing the love life of Fandango Fannie.[26] The chorus entered in a "gypsy wagon drawn by a cute little donkey," the first of several effects designed to replace the march as an entrance for the reduced

Corene Uzell (left) and Julia Lamaedrid in "In Old Mexico," The Daisy Dancers (1906). Corene Uzelle clipping file, Billy Rose Theater Collection, New York Public Library for the Performing Arts.

chorus.[27] Half the dancers were dressed as women, half as men. The "male" chorus wore white knee-length jodhpurs and long-sleeved sailor blouses; the dancers playing women wore white gored skirts, cut just below the knees, sailor blouses with bell sleeves that opened at the elbows, and corsets that produced the slender waist and "monobosom" of the era's ideal figure. Both groups wore white tights, sombreros, and the single strap, French heel shoe that was regulation footwear for dancers performing Wayburn's musical comedy technique.[28]

The dance performed by the chorus used ropes as hand props to connect the dancers. The ropes, which were at least ten feet long, were used as lassos, as an accessory for flirting, and for skipping rope. The last was a popular exercise for women, associated both with aesthetic calisthenics and with losing weight.[29]

In the second scene, "In Old Virginia," the chorus emerged "from a wigwam to execute a characteristic dance to Miss Jardon's solo of the Indian musical type."[30] Jardon's solo, "Pocohontas," was a comic song relating the courtship of the Indian "princess" and John Smith. It was filled with slapstick and puns like the following:

She said, "Papa let him live, he'll pay for all my grub,
He won't be home very much, he's joined an Indian club."

...

They were playing on a cliff, but Papa acted rough,
He pushed John Smith off the cliff but that was just a bluff.[31]

The Indian costumes worn by the chorus were all identical—dark tunics decorated with large diamond shapes.[32] The gender of the design cannot be determined from photographs.

Photographs are only slightly more helpful about the content of the dance. The clearest show the chorus seated "Indian-style" (with legs crossed in front) in a line parallel to the proscenium. The bodies of the dancers are placed at oblique right angles to the wigwam behind them at stage center. Each dancer leans toward the camera (and audience), balancing herself on her right hand and, with her left, shading her brow—a gesture that in the American Delsarte vocabulary meant either "hark!" or "I gaze into the distance."[33] Wayburn used similar formations, positions, and gestures in later "Indian" dance numbers, including an untitled scene with Will Rogers in the 1916 *Ziegfeld Midnight Frolics* and "Broadway Indians" from the *Ziegfeld Follies of 1922*.

The third scene in *The Daisy Dancers* was "In Old Japan." Its theme song, "My Little Lady of Japan," told a story similar to that of *Madame Butterfly*, which had recently been performed in New York. There was an important difference, however: the narrative voice in Wayburn's act—as opposed to Puccini's opera—was the American naval officer's, not his Japanese bride's.

The chorus of geishas and sailors wore kimonos and white flannel navy uniforms. The geishas had large, elaborate headdresses and Japanese fans that were more than two feet long; the sailors carried American flags. With these props, the dancers formed "picturesque groups in posings as...young men and maidens in courting couples dance to the rhythms of the melodious song."[34] Both the poses and the props recalled the flag and fan drills that had been popular in Chicago during Wayburn's adolescence. The set called for a "Japanese villa," but it is unclear whether this was a flat, a painted drop, or a three-dimensional structure.[35]

"In Daisyland," which closed the original version of the act, was extremely well received. In many reviews special mention was made of the costumes, set, and lighting; however, of the thirty-seven reviews pasted into Wayburn's scrapbooks, only two describe the dance and not a one mentions the ballad that accompanied the scene[36]—"Daisyland," by Jerome and Schwartz. The song was basically a utility number, in which the lyrics seldom matched the critical beats in the music with the critical points in the rhyme scheme.

The chorus costumes were similar to those illustrated in the Butterick book of fancy drills—a white dress decorated with clusters of artificial flowers in swags along the hem.[37] The sequined headdresses consisted of eighteen-petal fabric daisies, approximately sixteen inches in diameter, mounted on a pillbox band giving the effect of a mortarboard. Similar costumes may have been used in the "Awakening of the Daisies" scene of *Ned Wayburn's Girls of 1904*; in any case, he employed them again in many numbers, including "The Picnic March" transformation scene in *The Wife Hunters* (1912) and "Say it with Flowers" in *The Demi-Tasse Revue* (1920), a Capitol Theater Prolog.

"In Daisyland," insofar as the scene can be reconstructed, was a sequence of dazzling effects; the curtain opened on a set that "realistically depicted a daisy field bordering upon a small sheet of water with a woodland in the distance."[38] The background was painted to show a "crescent moon and moving clouds" above the trees.[39] It is likely that the set was constructed of three pieces—a backdrop, an elliptical painted or mirrored ground cloth representing the lake, and a practical hillside, raked to approximately five and one-half feet high, that was probably built from platforms like a three-dimensional prop rock.

Jardon began the scene with the song "Daisyland." At a signal, probably cued by the encore of the song's refrain, "the most novel and intricate electrical effects [were] shown, in which [the chorus dancers] [were] suddenly transformed into living daisies."[40] In the absence of a lighting plot, one can only speculate about what these effects were. Most likely, the chorus dancers were hidden under the hillside set piece in a way that left their daisy hats visible; then, on cue, they jumped through holes cut in the set—the technique used in "The Picnic March"—with their sequined headdresses reflecting the light.[41] To heighten the effect, a shower of daisies fell to the stage from a gutter system similar to that used in the storm scene in *The Rain-dears*.[42]

After this came a dance—probably a precision number in the style of the Original English Pony Ballet—performed by Jardon and the chorus with "spinning parasols" decorated with daisies.[43] The dance ended in a "striking tableau, with the star at the center, that commanded attention." Then, more "beautiful and bewildering electrical effects [were] displayed, during which the dancers disappear[ed], leaving a large flower,"[44] an illusion that could have been created by dimming all the lights except those that shone directly down on the daisy hats. Finally, as a critic noted, Jardon seemed to glide out from the large flower and disappear,[45] an exit that probably involved bourrées, the step typically used by ballerinas in spectacle shows to float offstage.

The popularity of the "Daisyland" effects was such that the order of the act was rearranged. By September 1906, "In Old Virginia" had been dropped. "Daisyland" now opened the act, followed by "In Old Japan," "In Old Mexico," and a new sequence, "a beautiful tableau" entitled "North and South."[46] The addition featured a new song, "The Yankee Boy in Blue," which was published by Jerome H. Remick and Company as the "musical number introduced by Ned Wayburn's Daisy Dancers." When a song of the period carried such an imprint, it was generally a sign that a show was so popular that the mere mention of the title would open the purse of potential buyers.

The song was composed by Dorothy Jardon and may have been included in the show at her insistence—as the prerogative of a star. But its inclusion may also have been a sign of Wayburn's own recognition of the increasing importance of a connective theme in feature acts: the lyrics describe the female narrator's love for "soldier [men] from Old Japan to sunny Mexico."[47] Bugle calls were integrated into the musical accompaniment.

Unfortunately, no photographs of the scene exist, and newspaper accounts say little more than that it represented "an army in camp."[48] It is likely, given the song and scene titles, that the tableau had a Civil War setting, but there are no references to the war in the lyrics.

Wayburn's experiments with feature acts helped him codify the theories and polish the skills that he called upon in his later career. He learned to manipulate groups of various sizes onstage and to use the manipulations to create a performance hierarchy. The themes that were important to these experiments will be discussed in the next two chapters.

Wayburn's vision of the integrated stage faced a major challenge in the 1910s from solo and duo specialty performers who insisted on interpolating their own acts into scripted shows and were backed by producers. As Wayburn recognized, this practice, if not handled properly, could destroy his control over shows, and he attempted to create structures that allowed for the integration of specialty acts into his choreography without destroying its overall design.[1] This chapter will examine how Wayburn incorporated individual "specialties" into musical comedies and revues. Although he worked with many kinds of specialty performers, including romantic and "character" singers, monologuists, comics, jugglers, and musicians, the discussion will focus on acts chiefly involving dance.

Wayburn used two basic methods to integrate dance specialties into musical comedies and revues—insertion and montage. The first allowed for a single specialty to be interpolated into a scene; the second brought three to ten specialty acts together in a show-within-a-show format. Wayburn used the montage system in unplotted revues throughout his career: the "Laceland" scene in the 1922 *Ziegfeld Follies*, for example, was a montage of individual specialties and chorus routines. The montage system was also frequently employed in the musical comedies and topical revues that Wayburn created for Lew Fields and the Shubert Brothers between 1909 and 1913, and in the shows that he produced for London music halls beginning in 1913. The two examples of the montage format that will be discussed in detail below—the Act I finale from *The Passing Show of 1913* and the "Escalade" act created for the London Hippodrome—both date from 1913.

The montage format served as a connecting link between the vaudeville feature acts of Wayburn's early career and the revues that were an important part of his later one. In its simplest form, a montage scene resembled the feature acts that he had produced for the New York Theater Roof shows, such as *Ned Wayburn's Girls of 1904*, which included seven solo specialties and four chorus numbers.

An early example of the technique was the Act II opener in *The Midnight Sons* (1909) designed by Arthur Voegtlin. Here, Wayburn worked an actual variety show into the scene, which depicted the interior of the Merri Murray Variety Theater—built by one of the "sons" for his actress girlfriend—down to the spectators, who faced the show's real audience.[2] The specialties featured in the montage were all based on turns or precision lines, both of which could be perceived from any angle. The line work was performed by the Original English Pony Ballet; the turns were provided by Rosalia Ceballos, performing on a single trapeze, and,

Rosalia Ceballos working the double rings in the Act II opening scene of The Midnight Sons *(1909). Lew Fields Scrapbook, Billy Rose Theater Collection, New York Public Library for the Performing Arts.*

depending on the date of performance, by the ballet-trained dancers Mazie King, Mabel Meeker, or Gladys Moore. King, who appeared in the production in New York, and Meeker and Moore, who danced in the show on tour, had all been compared to Adeline Genée, who, in the days before Anna Pavlova, was viewed in America as the world's greatest ballet dancer.[3]

In revues, the montage format was frequently used to accommodate specialties linked by topical reference rather than by design or movement style. The Harem Scene (Act I finale) in *The Passing Show of 1912* and "The Blushing Ballet" in the *Ziegfeld Follies of 1916*, for example, were both montages inspired by satires of Russian dancers. The Harem Scene also managed to satirize *Kismet*, *Sumurun*, popular plays such as *The Return of Peter Grimm* (by David Belasco) and *Poor Little Rich Girl* (by Eleanor Gates), as well as the melodrama *Bought and Paid For*. It featured a triple dose of comedienne Trixie Friganza, who parodied Anna Pavlova (twice), Gertrude Hoffmann, and the apache dance introduced by Maurice Mouvet and Florence Walton. With both Hoffmann and Mouvet soon to be featured in another Wayburn/Shubert production, *Broadway to Paris* (1912), the parody of their acts was publicity for the new show.

The Harem Scene ended with a performance by Anna Wheaton and George Moon of Louis A. Hirsch's "Bacchanale Rag." This song, a notable example of "ragging the classics," was a syncopated version of Alexander Glazunov's *Autumn Bacchanale*, to which Pavlova and Mikhail Mordkin had performed their most famous duet.[4] The lyrics acknowledged Hirsch's debt to his source:

> Take some music, start to fake some music in lag time,
> Syncopate it, hesitate it, then you have some rag-time;
> Steal from the masters any classic you see,
> Rag it a little bit with his melody;
> Don't try at all to hide, call it the Gaby Glide,
> No matter what it may be.
>
> Other writers will give brother writers inspiration,
> Handy Op'ra will be dandy, just for syncopation.
> …
>
> Play me that Bacchanale rag, dear,
> That musical daze, sways, plays with every feeling.[5]

An important element in the success of Wayburn's topical satires, regardless of format, was his accuracy in duplicating the iconography of the originals. In the case of Pavlova's *Bacchanale* and Wayburn's rag version of the dance, both the costumes and poses closely matched.

"The Blushing Ballet" in the 1916 edition of the *Ziegfeld Follies* was typical in its satirical treatment of Vaslav Nijinsky, the Ballets Russes star who had garnered most of the publicity during the company's American tour earlier in the year. A topical montage, the scene had the same format as its Harem Scene predecessor—several specialty acts satirizing a performer, work, or role. As in the Harem Scene, there was an element of overkill in the multiple parodies. The scene opened with excerpts from *Les Sylphides* (itself a montage of solos and duets framed by a female corps),[6] then went on to a parody of *Schéhérazade* featuring Ziegfeld's current slate of comics: the heavy-set Sam B. Hardy, who played the Sultan; the eccentric dancer Don Barclay as Zobéide (the ballet's femme fatale); tall Norman Blume as the Eunuch; W.C. Fields as O Pshaw (a pun that did not refer directly to a character in the ballet); and Bert Williams as "Le Nègre" (as Nijinsky's Golden Slave was renamed).[7] No script for the scene exists (none, in fact, was submitted to the United States Copyright Office with the rest of the *Follies* script), but one can assume that it parodied Nijinsky's bounding entrance, the harem atmosphere, and the climactic orgy.[8] The next act was by Carl Randall, a talented ballet-trained dancer, as Nijinsky in *Le Spectre de la Rose*. Although Fokine had choreographed the work as a duet, Randall's parody may have been a solo, since the best known elements of the original were Nijinsky's rose petal costume and his leap out the window at the end. If Randall did have a partner, it was probably Emma Haig, the soloist in *Les Sylphides*.

Finally, Fanny Brice entered. Dressed in harem pants and a bandeau recalling Nijinsky's costume in *Schéhérazade*, she sang Gene Buck's

"Nijinsky." Unlike "The Bacchanale Rag," the song contained no musical references. Its lyrics, however, were satirical—and very funny:

> He's a guiding star, owns a motor car, pals with the Czar, they say.
> His gymnastical style, beats the Castles a mile.
> His fantastical smile has won my heart away.
> …
> He does Petroushka and gets the cushka,
> His ballet wayski's won my love.
> And I am gonski, when he does the Faunski.
> I like Nijinsky because he's airy like, and fairy like, and very like a Dove.[9]

The scene ended with Brice singing with the male chorus, described by one critic as "a whole stage of Bunthorne-like Nijinskys."[10] The costume in the Ballets Russes repertory most like that of Gilbert and Sullivan's aesthete Bunthorne was the Poet's in *Les Sylphides*—a black tunic with white tights, a white blouse with flowing sleeves and a large, limp bow, and a shoulder-length blonde wig. It is likely, therefore, that "The Blushing Ballet" ended, as it had begun, with a parody of *Les Sylphides*, a work that frequently opened Ballets Russes programs.[11]

The Act I finale of *The Passing Show of 1913* also used the montage format. In this scene, "The Capitol Steps," the specialty numbers were closely linked to the revue's plot—the capturing of the presidency from Woodrow Wilson by a suffragist leader, "Mrs. George Monroe Potiphar Crankhurst." The scene hinged on two sets of allusions: the reaction of real politicians and theatrical figures to this feminist "nightmare" and the National American Suffrage Association's election eve pageant *The Allegory*, which was staged on the Treasury Building steps by Hazel MacKaye on 3 March 1913.[12] Although there is no evidence that Wayburn or scriptwriter Harold Atteridge attended the pageant, it was extensively reported in the New York press.

The set, one of the few designed by Wayburn and credited to him, represented the facade of the United States Capitol in Washington, D.C., where presidents were traditionally inaugurated. Like the actual building, the set was dominated by steps where much of the action took place, as in *The Allegory*. Wayburn, who had worked as an architectural draftsman at the Chicago World's Fair, was familiar with the classical revival style of American architecture, of which the Capitol was a prime example. To recreate its famous staircase, he foreshortened the dimensions of the original, narrowing the steps by almost fifty percent. The final structure, which consisted of thirty-four steps, reached to the rear of the stage and rose to almost three-quarters of the height of the Winter Garden Theater. About halfway up the staircase on each side were platforms and balconies with obelisks. The staircase covered the middle two-thirds of the stage at its lowest step, which was placed about five feet back from the proscenium. Since Wayburn had designed the set himself, it can be assumed that he built the staircase with risers no higher than a comfortable seven-and-a-half inches.[13]

Specialty and chorus dancers used every possible area of the set, from the apron in front of the staircase to the platform at its apex, the two balconies, and all the steps. The movement direction for each act's routine was different from the preceding one.

The running order of the scene, as best as can be reconstructed from scripts, programs, and reviews, was as follows:

"The March of the North, East, South and West"	Chorus
"The White House Glide"	Bessie Clayton and Ballet
"The Ballet Girl"	Charlotte Greenwood
"Zatum"	Swan Wood
"The Golden Stairs of Love"	Wellington Cross and Lois Josephine
"Tangle-Footed Monkey Wrench"	Carter de Haven and Fred Nice, Jr.
"Inauguration Day"	Corene Frances and Chorus[14]

The scene, which began after the seizing of the Woodrow Wilson government, ended with Mrs. George Monroe Potiphar Crankhurst's inauguration as President. Her name alone revealed the script's antagonism to feminism: "Crankhurst" was a play on the surname of the British suffragette leader, Mrs. Emmeline Pankhurst, who had toured the United States in 1912; George Monroe was a female impersonator whose best known characterization was a fat, obnoxious Irish cook; Potiphar was a reference to the Biblical seducer of Joseph.[15] The scene also satirized Wilson's unpopular domestic policies, Marc Antony's funeral oration from Shakespeare's *Julius Caesar*, and the building mania of various public figures.

The opening march, by Louis A. Hirsch, accompanied a dance number for the female chorus employing Wayburn's musical comedy idiom. Four columns of dancers entered from the two balconies and from the platform at the top of the staircase. After a sixteen-measure introduction, each column marched down the steps to a different musical theme.[16] No lyrics for this march have been found, and it is possible that none were used.

The first solo specialty was an eccentric ballet by Bessie Clayton, backed by an eight-woman chorus. Clayton was a well-known dancer who had been a member of the Lew Fields company, but as far as it is possible to ascertain, this was the first time she had worked with Wayburn. She had made her stage debut in 1899 and had earned her reputation from the strength and endurance of her pointework. Critics reviewing her performance in *The Passing Show of 1913* described her "perennial pirouetting" as "break-bone toe dancing."[17]

In "The Capitol Steps" she had to move down the staircase in one of two ways—either in a series of piqué turns or in a series of pendulum kicks. The pendulum kick, a trademark of toe tapping, was a sequence of hops, with the working leg moving from front to back.[18] In both steps, a single movement was performed on each tread of the staircase and took up one unit of rhythm (a beat or a measure depending on the tempo). Both steps were performed at oblique angles to the audience along a slightly diagonal path. Staircase toe specialties were traditionally solos, so it is unlikely that the ballet chorus also performed on the steps; instead, they probably remained on the balconies during Clayton's routine.

It is not known who actually choreographed Clayton's solo. Clayton herself claimed that she had invented the staircase dance in Vienna in 1912.[19] Mazie King, her replacement when the show went on tour, also claimed to have originated the dance. Indeed, even before 1913, she frequently toe-tapped down the staircases of landmark towers and buildings as a publicity stunt.[20]

The cue for Clayton's act was the parody of a line from Marc Antony's funeral oration from *Julius Caesar*: "And I'll send for Julius Harberger, the sheriff from New York and then watch Mrs. Crankhurst howl. For we'll let Julius seize her."[21] May Boley, who played Mrs. Crankhurst, then ran down the staircase followed by the male chorus of soldiers and policemen. As they reached the bottom, Clayton appeared at the top of the staircase to begin her number.

A parody of Clayton's number by the long-legged comedienne Charlotte Greenwood immediately followed. Instant debunking was a device that Wayburn frequently used in shows with a montage format; he also used it when choreographing around inserted acts, as will be seen below in the discussion of Vanda Hoff's nautch dance.

Greenwood performed on the apron of the stage rather than on the staircase. Since her name was on the list of performers specially insured to work on the steps, it is likely that she simply could not negotiate them. No score or sheet music for her number was published, but, since the theme of the girl who wanted to become a ballet dancer was so common in theatrical and popular music, it is possible that the song was pulled out of "stock" or created for Greenwood's vaudeville act, which ran from 1911 to 1913.[22]

The next item, "Zatum," was performed by Swan Wood in the center of the staircase. Wood was a dancer whose specialties ranged from eccentric and acrobatic ballet to a solo that she called "The Whirling Dervish Sword Dance." She had studied both in Paris in 1900—ballet with one Madame Bordoni of the Opéra and whirling dervish technique with Hadji Sheriffe, who was then appearing at the Paris Exposition. Although costumed in a beaded version of the brassiere and skirt generally associated with vaudeville Salomés, Wood claimed that the number was a minute-and-a-half excerpt from an authentic dervish dance.[23] There is simply not enough evidence to verify or dispute her claim.

Wellington Cross and Lois Josephine, an exhibition ballroom team, performed the next specialty, "The Golden Stairs of Love." The pair had

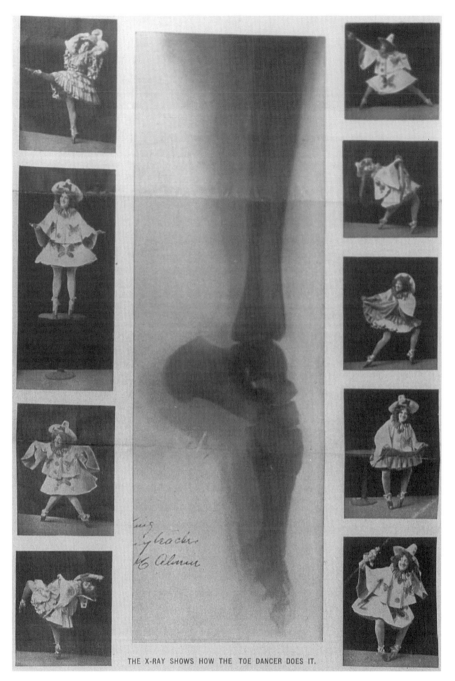

THE X-RAY SHOWS HOW THE TOE DANCER DOES IT.

An X-ray of Mazie King's foot and ankle with photographs showing her in poses from an eccentric ballet solo, 1899. Mazie King clipping file, Billy Rose Theater Collection, New York Public Library for the Performing Arts.

worked together for three years and was very popular in vaudeville; they saw *The Passing Show* as an opportunity to demonstrate that they could handle dialogue as well as dance. The characters they played—Never-Say-

Die [i.e. William] Collier and the Sunshine Girl—were involved in most of the plot, although in "The Capitol Steps" their dialogue was little more than a romantic prelude to the song.

During the song, they performed an "Innovation"—a hesitation two-step done in a "butterfly" pose, that is, facing each other with their arms stretched to the side. The Innovation was frequently used in theatrical choreography since it was the only social dance in which the partners did not actually touch. In this scene, Cross began the dance at the foot of the staircase, while Josephine entered from behind the balustrade on the left balcony. Their positions on the steps were defined by the lyrics of the song. At three critical points in the song's rhyme scheme, the male narrator crooned about "climbing" to reach the woman:

> Way up in the sky, [you're]way up there so high,
> If I want you, dear, then Love's stairs I will climb,
> Each step at a time, 'til you find me near.
> I'll climb to you, if you'll be true.
> While love bells chime, to you I'll climb.[24]

When an Innovation was used in theatrical choreography, the number generally ended with the couple touching for the first time. In "The Golden Stairs of Love," the song's musical climax occurred just as Cross climbed to the balustrade where Josephine had entered, so it is likely that the couple exited from this balcony, instead of returning to the bottom of the staircase.

The scene's final specialty number was the "Tangle-Footed Monkey Wrench," performed by the tandem team of Carter de Haven and Fred Nice, Jr.[25] De Haven was best known as a vaudeville comic and a juvenile lead, especially in acts that he performed with his wife, Flora Parker. Fred Nice, Jr., by contrast, was making the transition from a career as an eccentric comic to one as an adagio dance partner to Ada May Weeks.[26] The tandem techniques of shadowing and mirroring, which will be discussed below, could only have been used at the beginning of the number, since the "tangle-footed" falls used elsewhere were eccentric, "characterizational" movements, like the pitching in "boat deck" acts or the staggering in "drunk" dances.

The integration of this number into "The Capitol Steps" was typical of Wayburn's work with casts that included both dancers and nondancers. The script began with a discussion of the architectural merits of the Capitol by New York Mayor William Jay Gaynor and producers David Belasco and Oscar Hammerstein, all known for commissioning expensive and elaborate buildings. The conversation ended with each saying, "Let us take a firm hand," after which the speaker tumbled down the stairs.[27] As in the Clayton specialty, the dancers made their entrance at the top of the staircase just as the actors playing Belasco, Gaynor, and Hammerstein reached the bottom.

The finale, "Inauguration Day," involved the scene's entire cast. The

Carter de Haven and Fred Nice, Jr., in "rube" outfits, performing tandem mirror work (LEFT) *and shadowing work. Fred Nice, Jr. photograph file, Billy Rose Theater Collection, New York Public Library for the Performing Arts.*

seven soloists and forty-eight female dancers tapped, while the male chorus, which did not dance, lined the edge of the staircase. Since the march music lasted at least 192 bars, it is likely that the specialty performers did brief encores during the finale.[28] The reviews describe rows of dancers tapping down the staircase in lines, but most photographs show the forty-eight women of the chorus in V-formations. Typically, the pictures depict a V created by four lines stretching from the stage floor to the level of the balustrades or covering the entire staircase. One photograph shows half the chorus in a single-file V, with each dancer placed on the step above her next-in-line. The other half of the chorus is lined up along the bottom step parallel to the proscenium.[29]

Wayburn's happiness at the enormous critical and popular success of "The Capitol Steps" was dampened somewhat by the knowledge that London-based producers were planning to steal the concept and reproduce the set without his permission. He therefore accepted an offer from Albert de Courville, manager of the London Hippodrome, and sailed for England. He and de Courville managed to open their version of "The Capitol Steps," called "Escalade, or the Magic Staircase," before their rivals, but they were so pressed for time that they missed the Hippodrome's regular Monday opening and premiered the scene on Tuesday, 30 September 1913.[30]

"Escalade," unlike "The Capitol Steps," was a music hall (or vaudeville) act; it dropped the New York jokes and did not have a plot, although it retained the montage format. The number opened and closed with chorus marches, and included two specialties—a toe tapping solo by Mazie King and an eccentric comic dance by Willie Solar that featured the tripping-down-the-stairs effect of the de Haven and Nice duet from *The Passing Show*. The choruses may have been enlarged for one of the marches; forty-eight dancers are shown in most photographs, although one picture lends credence to the "seventy young women" mentioned by the critic of the *New York Morning Telegraph*.[31] As in *The Passing Show*, the chorus did one march in identical costumes and the other in "characterizational" dress.

The chorus patterns in "Escalade" were simpler than those in "The Capitol Steps." Most of the surviving photographs show four or five lines of twelve coming down the staircase parallel to the proscenium—a much more basic formation than the V.[32] The half-tone published in *The Graphic*, however, depicts a very complex grouping, based on X's. The bottom X was formed of two lines of twelve that reached all the way up to the balustrades, where twelve dancers stood in a straight line. Above this was a smaller X made up of two lines of six. From the center of this X to that of the larger one was another line of six dancers.[33]

* * *

Wayburn began working with the insertion method around 1907 and used it regularly until well into the 1920s. The system enabled him to interpolate specialty acts into musical comedies and revues without interrupting the stage action. The most commonly inserted acts were those derived from ballroom and "characterizational" dances. In both types of acts, elaborate masking devices were sometimes used to create a rationale for the specialty; at other times, however, there was simply the cue, "Let's dance."

The specialty acts derived from ballroom forms were based on the footwork and positions of dances popular between 1906 and 1918. The acts most often inserted into Wayburn shows, and those that will be discussed below, were one-steps, tangos, whirlwinds, and tandem work.

The structure of Wayburn's ballroom-derived specialties varied little over his stage career. Each act followed the extended routine format—a romantic or flirtatious ballad for a single voice (usually male), the dance itself, and, as a finale, a repeat by all the performers of the ballad's refrain. The acts were generally located within settings where social dancing might take place: the specialties in *The Midnight Sons* (1909), for example, were set in a garden fete at the "Pounceuponham Hotel, Billionaire Beach, Florida."[34]

In order to differentiate the theatrical versions of these specialties from their ballroom originals, Wayburn used many devices to make his interpolated one-steps and tangos unique. Poses were frequently exaggerated, especially those employing "butterfly" and Les-a-Cote holds, in which the arms were outstretched. In the Gaby Glide, the history of which will be explained below, Gaby Deslys held her partner, Harry Pilcer, in a variant of the "butterfly" that distinctly resembled a half-nelson stranglehold. She stood in front of him: he clasped her right arm behind her back, while she hooked her left arm backward around his neck.[35]

Wayburn also made his social dance specialties unique by setting them in a characterizational mode. One way he did this was through "eccentric" casting. His most common method, especially after *Town Topics* (1915), in which five teams of dancers appeared, was to pair a tall man with a short woman. Thus, lanky Clifton Webb and petite Mary Hay, who had both appeared as solo eccentric dancers in Wayburn shows, were teamed together to create one of the period's best known duo acts.

Two basic comedy strategies were used in these inserted eccentric acts. "New teams" often pretended that they had just met and were trying to work out the problems of dancing together for the first time, a narrative device used later in the Fred Astaire-Ginger Rogers films. Established teams were frequently dressed in "rube" outfits—comic versions of unsophisticated country wear— with hats that emphasized the difference in the partners' heights. In either case, the basic comedy step involved the man performing a hitch, side, or fan kick over the woman's head.

In musical comedies, especially those created in the early 1920s, the female specialty lead was often teamed with the eccentric comic male for a short dance; after this, she performed with the romantic lead in a ballroom or cabaret setting. In *Two Little Girls in Blue* (1921), Evelyn Law and Jack Donahue did a reprise of her solo, "There's Something About Me They Like," as a duet. Three moments from this dance can be identified. In the first, a supported arabesque in a modified "butterfly" position, he held her working foot with his left hand while clasping her right hand with his free hand. At the cli-

Jack Donahue and Evelyn Law in the final pose of an eccentric whirlwind in Two Little Girls in Blue *(1921). Billy Rose Theater Collection, New York Public Library for the Performing Arts.*

max, he did hitch kicks over her head, and, since these were also Law's solo specialty, she performed them over his kneeling body as well.[36] A photograph of the final pose shows her draped across his shoulders in a lift.

Duos for a "rube" and a sophisticate or for an "American" (or standard ballroom dancer) and a Russian were other social dance specialties that used characterizational material. Depending on the season, the Russian could be a woman dancing on pointe or a man doing the *kazachok*.[37] In either case, the dialogue or pantomime immediately preceding the dance was flirtatious. Another specialty that was easily inserted into musical comedies was the "drunk dance," in which the male partner did a drunk act. This specialty, associated with Vernon Castle before he left Lew Fields and took up exhibition ballroom dancing, consisted of a conventional one-step or hesitation walk, with sways, dips, and trip steps that suggested a man in his cups.

Another technique that distinguished Wayburn's specialty acts from ballroom styles was the use of props or accessories. These were especially prevalent in dances based on Innovations (because the couple, not having to touch, had their hands free) and one-steps with Les-a-Cote holds, in which each dancer held only one of his partner's hands. In *Town Topics* (1915), Cross and Josephine, for example, did an Innovation holding an umbrella, while in *The Passing Show of 1912*, Adelaide and Hughes performed a hesitation waltz with a hoop that extended their arms and connected their bodies.[38]

Wayburn sometimes created named social dances to publicize featured performers in a show. Generally, these dances were not new, nor were they particularly innovative; they were designed, rather, to create publicity. The names sometimes contained topical references—the case of "The Bacchanale Rag," for instance. Typically, the choreography was based on conventional steps with added poses that parodied the source. Thus, in "The Galli-Curci Rag" and "My Sist' Tetrazzini"—both from 1913 and named after celebrated opera singers—the dancers clasped their hands to the diaphragm in a parody of diva performance behavior.

Dances named for the women who created them were almost always glides, since the step for which the dance was named was performed with the woman in front of the man. Since these glides were commissioned for specific acts or shows, the lyrics often included information about the performers. For example, the "Gertrude Hoffmann Glide," created for Hoffmann's starring vehicle *Broadway to Paris* (1912), alluded to her vaudeville imitation act, "The Borrowed Art of Gertrude Hoffmann":

> Come take the Raggy motion of the Gaby Glide,
> Try a dash of Salome;
> Keep on sliding and sliding
> And in the Spring Song, do the trot's gone home.
> O, take the speedy go you find in Georgie Cohan,

Use the grace with which the Russians slide.
Then to Eva Tanguay shout "Oh gee, I don't care,"
Just give me the Gertrude Hoffmann Glide.[39]

The Gaby Glide, mentioned in the first line of the refrain (and in "The Bacchanale Rag" verse), serves as an interesting example of Wayburn's more self-conscious use of the insertion technique. The dance was named for the French music hall star, Gaby Deslys, imported by the Shuberts to star in their Winter Garden show *Vera Violette* (1912). Since Deslys was better known for her romantic exploits than her dancing skills, the Shuberts sent her to the Wayburn studio, where he assigned her to work with the exhibition dancer Harry Pilcer.[40]

Because Pilcer wrote the accompanying song and also performed it, the lyrics offer even more information than usual about the dance. The refrain, for instance, included the line, "Do the side step, trip, then go back on the other [foot]," which describes a step from the Maurice Tango. In her book *The Tango and How To Do It*, Dorothy Crozier explains the sequence in slightly greater detail: the dancers "step forward on their left feet, bring right [foot] to the heel of the left, at the same time kicking left [foot] forward, then bring left to instep of right."[41]

Pilcer performed "The Gaby Glide" with a female chorus, not with Deslys. However, in 1912 when the two went to Paris, they introduced a dance that she called the "Deedle-dum-dee."[42] Variously described as a Grizzly Bear, Turkey Trot, and Castle Walk, the number may have been a glide. On returning to New York the following year, Deslys and Pilcer joined the cast of Wayburn's show *The Honeymoon Express*. Interpolated as a publicity stunt, their song and dance number, "When Gaby Did the Gaby Glide," was the only one that Wayburn (not Pilcer) received credit for staging. The device he used to insert the number into the plot was transparent. Pilcer, as the character Baudy, discovers that the woman he has promised to dance with in an earlier scene is actually the "boy" (Deslys in trousers) with whom he is now conversing. She tells him that he can have the dance if he makes it a Turkey Trot, and they begin to dance.[43] That Pilcer and Deslys had to break character to introduce their own theme dance does not seem to have bothered the critics.[44]

Two ballroom-derived specialties that frequently appeared in Wayburn shows were whirlwind and tandem dance numbers. Whirlwind dances, which were actually one-steps or waltzes that ended in a whirlwind turn, were popular in the years before the First World War. The turn itself was a combination of three spinning movements. Beginning in the standard waltz position, the couple faced each other, with the man's feet placed outside the woman's. The couple began to spin, straightening and extending their arms until they were leaning away from each other. Finally, the woman was whirled into the air by the man. In this way, three turns were made without a break in the motion. The whirlwind could end in one of three poses: with the couple standing next to each other in a Les-a-Cote position (suitable for young romantic teams such as Cross and Josephine); with the woman spun up to the man's shoulder (typical of Adelaide and Hughes); or with the man holding the woman by her waist as she plunged into a backbend over his bent knee (a position favored by the Marvelous Millers).[45]

Wayburn frequently staged whirlwinds for eccentric and acrobatic dance teams as well as for romantic pairs like Adelaide and Hughes or Wellington and Cross. Tall, eccentric male comics could spin short female partners to their shoulders with great effect. Wayburn's first known use of the whirlwind was in his choreography for a brother and sister acrobatic team, Hilarion and Rosalia Ceballos (of the Mexican circus family). The dance, which he inserted in *The Phantastic Phantoms* (1907), featured unique additions to the one-step vocabulary: not only did Rosalia Ceballos cartwheel to stage center to begin the dance, but she also challenged convention by spinning her taller brother in the whirlwind.[46]

There were a number of similarities between whirlwind dances and apaches. The vocabulary was close, and each involved a male dancer spinning his female partner. However, unlike the plotted apache (which climaxed in stylized murder), whirlwind dances had no characterizational elements.

The final duet specialty that Wayburn inserted into shows was tandem work. Always performed by dancers of the same sex, it derived from the Innovation and Les-a-Cote type of one-steps. Although tandem teams could work in Wayburn's musical comedy, tap, acrobatics, or modern Americanized ballet idioms, the poses and holds were indistinguishable from those employed in ballroom specialties.

The popularity of tandem work in the United States can be traced to the appearances of the English team of Moon and Morris in vaudeville and in *The Passing Show of 1912*. The team specialized in shadow work performed in a glide position: that is, the dancers stood in front of one another, while executing identical movements simultaneously.

Although Moon and Morris did not look alike—Morris was almost a head taller than his partner—Wayburn consistently adapted tandem techniques for teams of identical twins. The concept of identical dancers was important to Wayburn, possibly as a link between the precision ensembles inspired by the Original English Pony Ballet and the large tap choruses of his Prologs.

A tandem team for which Wayburn created many specialties was that of Madeline and Marion Fairbanks, known as the Fairbanks or the Thankhauser Twins. These young women, who had worked with Wayburn as children in *The Jolly Bachelors* (1910), returned to the New York stage in 1917 after four years in films. They did tandem work in many Wayburn shows, including the *Ziegfeld Follies* of 1917, 1918, and 1919, a Prolog entitled *Makin' Believe* (1923), and the musical comedy *Two Little Girls in Blue* (1921), which was written especially for them. The Fairbanks Twins used both shadowing and mirroring devices in their numbers. One of their first tandems for Wayburn was a mirror dance in the *Ziegfeld Follies of 1918*. The scene was called "A Miniature": here, wrote *The New York Globe*, "the dainty little Fairbanks Twins, dancing on either side of an imaginary mirror, seem to reflect each other, the song ["When I'm Looking at You"] rendered by Lillian Lorraine [being] simulated at the other side of the mirror by a young lady [Marie Wilson] from the troupe."[47] Mirroring devices also appeared in their numbers for two other *Follies* shows: in the 1917 *Follies*, they played the Army and the Navy in a patriotic number, while in the 1919 edition, they were Salt and Pepper in the "Follies Salad" scene. Both numbers had tap work, so that, in addition to reflecting each other's movements, the dancers had to achieve absolute precision in the timing of their steps.

Madeleine and Marion Fairbanks taking a curtain call for "A Miniature," Ziegfeld Follies of 1918. Fairbanks Twins photograph file, Billy Rose Theater Collection, New York Public Library for the Performing Arts.

The couple's mirror and shadow work was the inspiration behind *Two Little Girls in Blue* (1921), remembered today as Ira Gershwin's first show. In fact, as a vehicle for their specialties, the show was the ultimate tandem act. The plot, which concerned a pair of identical twins who illegally share a cabin on a cruise ship by pretending to be one girl, was built around a series of mirroring dances. Wayburn included both real and illusionary numbers, devising a traditional mirror act (similar to that in the 1918 *Follies*); a real mirror act (performed by one of the twins with a genuine reflecting glass while the other twin was offstage); and, finally, a dance for both sisters that was performed in a room filled with mirrors.[48]

Wayburn used shadow work in *Two Little Girls in Blue* only when both twins were onstage—in the scenes set in their cabin, in the finale, and in the opening scene, which showed the various passengers boarding the ship. Here, Wayburn inserted short specialty numbers for Evelyn Law, Vanda Hoff, and Jack Donahue, while choreographing shadow numbers for both the Fairbanks sisters and the male Towson Twins, who played the ship's stewards.[49]

Solo specialty dances were the acts most frequently inserted into shows. They were also the easiest to interpolate. Most were standard routines performed in the eccentric mode of one of Wayburn's codified techniques—musical comedy, tap and stepping, acrobatics, and modern Americanized ballet. Solo specialties could be performed by the dancer alone onstage, or they could be framed by the chorus.

Wayburn created literally hundreds of these specialties during the twenty-three most productive years of his career. His Arabian acrobatic solos and Hawaiian hula solos—two of his many forays into exotica— exemplified his use of this specialty. The first group, a hodgepodge of Egyptian, Turkish, Persian, and Indian styles, included both serious numbers and parodies. Wayburn used comics and specialty dancers in the parodies, most of which concerned Jewish women from New York's Lower East Side who wanted to become Egyptian dancers. Accompanying these specialties was a genre of satirical songs, the most famous of which were written by Harold Atteridge, Irving Berlin, and Blanche Merrill for Fanny Brice. Known collectively as "Sadie Songs" (from Berlin's "Sadie Salome, Go Home"), the genre was popular between 1909, when Salomania was at its height, and 1916, when Brice switched to "Becky Songs."[50]

The more serious Arabian soloists, however, did not impose Broadway references on their vision of the Middle East. Although their solos may not have been especially accurate, they were no less authentic than the nautch dances performed at the time by Ruth St. Denis. Indeed, many of Wayburn's Arabian soloists were concert dancers, including Evan Burrows-Fontaine (appearing in *The Ed Wynn Carnival*, 1920), Vanda Hoff (*Two Little Girls in Blue*, 1921), and Florence O'Denishawn (*Hitchy-Koo of 1920*), who, as her name suggests, was trained by St. Denis and Ted Shawn.

The degree and form of integration varied with the show. Burrows-Fontaine, working in an unplotted revue, simply performed her act with a chorus. The solo was Egyptian in terms of costume and gesture and had a specially designed set that reproduced the base of a sphinx. O'Denishawn, who appeared in a montage type scene entitled "The History of Dance," performed an Arabian solo that Shawn had created for her two years earlier, except that now it was surrounded by a "Chinese" set.[51] Hoff, playing an Indian stowaway, did an acrobatic solo that Heywood Broun described as "the farthest nautch of the season."[52] Although her number was fully integrated into the script, it was treated like an insertion. During the curtain call that followed her second encore, Hoff concealed herself under a full-length veil. Jack Donahue, the eccentric dancer and comic, replaced her under her veil, then threw it off, and launched into a parody of her dance.[53] This instant debunking was typical of Wayburn's work with exotic solos and recalls his use of multiple satires in montage scenes.

The hula, whether identified as Hawaiian, Polynesian, Javanese, or coming from the South Seas, was chronologically the last type of individual specialty that Wayburn incorporated into his shows. The dance, popular from the mid-1910s to the early 1920s, bore little relation to the ritual dances of the Pacific Islands. Basically, it was a shimmy with waving arms.[54]

Popular from the mid-1910s to the late 1920s, the shimmy was characterized by a rapid shaking of the shoulders, or "shimmy shakes."[55] The dance derived from a French version of the Grizzly Bear, in which shoulder movements were added to the swaying torso of the one-step, and from "La Java," in which the hips were shaken on syncopated offbeats.[56] Although there were dozens of explanations for the origin of the word "shimmy," Gilda Gray's suggestion that it was a slang term for chemise (or slip) seems most likely. Certainly, it was the favorite explanation of Broadway and Tin Pan Alley lyricists, as in this couplet written for Eddie Cantor:

I asked a girl to Shimmy and she said "by gosh,
How can I do the Shimmy when it's in the wash."[57]

The craze for Hawaiian music and dance, it has been said, began with play *The Bird of Paradise*, which premiered in 1912 and was revived in 1916.[58] The large number of travelogues and books on the Pacific Islands also contributed to interest in the hula.[59] Wayburn staged many Hawaiian and South Seas dance acts, including "I Left Her on the Beach at Honolulu" (*Ziegfeld Follies of 1916*), "Luana Lou" (*Ziegfeld Midnight Frolics* and *Ned Wayburn's Girlie Gambols*, both 1916), and "'Neath the South Sea Moon" (*Ziegfeld Follies of 1922*). All of these acts was based on the extended routine format and included both a song and a dance specialty that was inserted into the revue.

The songs on which these numbers were based were quite similar, which is not surprising since they all had lyrics by Gene Buck and music by Louis A. Hirsch, Dave Stamper, or both. Each song was nostalgic, with a male singer recalling a past romance with a Hawaiian dancer. The "Luana Lou" refrain began with the title words sung over the progression E F A D (associated with the song "Aloha Ai"), followed by syncopation. "I Left Her on the Beach at Honolulu" was a conventional ragtime, with accents on the first and fourth beats, and a refrain using seconds and minor thirds. "'Neath the South Sea Moon" was the most romantic of the three songs. Its surrounding scene, "A Hawaiian Tourist," featured extensive dialogue, a male and a female tourist, a Hawaiian dancer (Gilda Gray), and choruses of Hawaiians and mainlanders.

The settings for "I Left Her on the Beach at Honolulu" and "'Neath the South Sea Moon" were virtually identical—palm trees designed by Joseph Urban.[60] The choreography was also similar, featuring in each case a chorus of twenty-four that performed a barefoot hula, then draped itself in a shallow semicircle. In the first act, vocalist John Steele sang the ballad to Ann Pennington; in the second, Barnard Granville sang to mainlander Ina Claire while Gilda Gray danced.

For various reasons "Luana Lou" had a somewhat different format.

When the act was staged for the *Midnight Frolics*, it was played on a staircase, not a flat stage. Also affecting the choreography was the casting: the lead hula dancers were played by the Dolly Sisters, who specialized in tandem work. In "Luana Lou" they did mirror work, but performed the movements at oblique angles to each other (and to the proscenium), thus forming a V. This V could easily be emphasized in hula shimmy dancing, which depended on sideways movements of the outside legs and hips. The choreography for "I Left Her on the Beach in Honolulu" was typical of the musical comedy and tap routines that Wayburn had previously staged for Pennington and featured all her signature movements, including the sideways lunge.

Gilda Gray's "South Sea Dance" was notated by Wayburn's student Byrne MacFadden and published in *Dance Lovers Magazine* in 1924. Although Gray claimed that each performance of the dance was divinely inspired, there is little doubt that the act itself was choreographed by Wayburn. Like Pennington's dance, Gray's was in strict routine format, with all the identifiable elements of Wayburn's musical comedy choreography, including the repetition of steps, the emphasis on oblique angles, and the use of step turns. The "Oriental" turn that MacFadden describes, for example, was simply a Wayburn step turn performed to sixteen directions rather than the usual four or eight. Speaking in Gray's voice, she described the sequence as a

> pivot on the left foot [while you] push yourself around with the right. The right foot touches the floor at every beat of the music, and, as it does so, the left knee pliés, or bends in other words. When I do this turn I "shimmy my hips" at the same time....Do this turn for eight counts to the right, then reverse and do it for eight counts to the left.[61]

The previous chapter examined the methods used by Wayburn to incorporate individual specialty acts into musical comedies and revues. This chapter will study how he integrated specialty acts for chorus groups into the stage action of various kinds of shows. Because these acts depended upon the manipulation of large numbers of dancers, Wayburn divided the chorus into smaller, "specialized" units of six to twenty-four. This "differentiated" chorus prompted some of his most innovative choreography.

In the early 1900s, as we have said, the female chorus was classified by height, which was the distinction used to establish gender representation, and by the ability to dance on pointe. This system, inherited from nineteenth-century spectacle ballets, lasted on Broadway for decades. Wayburn, however, rejected it.

Instead, he substituted a system based on a variety of factors, including height and physical proportions, scale of movement, and the ability to perform his standard techniques—musical comedy, tap and stepping, acrobatics, modern Americanized ballet, and, to a lesser extent, exhibition ballroom dancing. Among the factors encouraging Wayburn's development of the new system was the increased length of revues, the larger pool of dancers available to him, and the codification of the techniques employed in his choreography.

The evolution of Wayburn's ideas about the chorus can be seen in two shows from the 1911–1912 season. *The Wife Hunters*, produced in November 1911, was probably his last show using the nineteenth-century system. In the Act I chorus number "My Little Havana Made" (the song referred to a cigar), the twenty-four dancers—six men and eighteen women—were arranged in a double semicircle. The six tallest women, in long dresses, were partnered by the six men, who wore knickers and shirts. The six shortest women danced with the remaining six women, who were dressed *en travesti* in elaborate Cuban boleros and jodhpurs. The casting and costuming were typical of Wayburn's work at the beginning of the decade. So, too was the chorus, which was differentiated by height and both real and assumed gender.

However, in *The Passing Show of 1912*, which premiered only seven months later, Wayburn divided the female chorus into three groups that were differentiated by the specialty techniques they performed. In the "Harem Scene," he filled the stage with two groups of exotic harem girls, dressed each group in a different costume, and added a chorus of eight that did a ballet number to Trixie Friganza's Pavlova imitation. Another sextet, led by Ida Schaall, performed diving tricks, plunging into an onstage pool.[1] The small male chorus played eunuchs. A photograph of

John Parks and chorus in "My Little Havana Made," The Wife Hunters (1911).
John Parks unmounted clipping file, Robinson Locke Collection, Billy Rose Theater
Collection, New York Public Library for the Performing Arts.

"The Bacchanale Rag" (in which Anna Wheaton did her Pavlova imitation) depicts this early example of the differentiated chorus. The divers are in back, standing on the highest platform, while the shortest dancers are hidden behind veils in the downstage area. The ballet dancers are not shown.

During World War I, many revues and musical comedies featured large female "soldier" choruses. Since these choruses typically did precision tap work (either of the conventional or toe tapping variety), the dancers needed considerable time together to rehearse. Since this took them away from general chorus rehearsals, precision dancers became known as a specialty chorus. Later in the decade, acrobatic choruses were employed; similarly, between the mid-1910s and the early 1920s, differentiated groups working in Arabian and hula styles were used. Throughout the period, however, a large contingent of female dancers continued to work solely in musical comedy technique.

Although many variations existed, Wayburn's chorus work relied on two basic physical patterns—the formation and the frame. Formations were the geometric shapes created by the dancers from their placement onstage. The configurations were designed to be completely visible only from above, rather than from an ideal viewing position in the first balcony.[2] However, since Wayburn seldom worked on a flat stage, his formations could be appreciated to some extent by the entire audience. The most commonly used configurations were rectangles, rhomboids, and parallelograms (as in Wayburn's early feature acts), circles, ovals, and ellipses, inverted V's and straight lines.

When used as a frame, the chorus was placed onstage in such a way as to focus attention on the soloists. The dancers were most frequently deployed in semicircles, inverted C's, V's, W's, or straight lines. In frame work, the chorus was used as a scenic element, delimiting the stage space and defining the audience's focus.

Unlike the female chorus, the male chorus, which typically numbered twelve, sixteen, or twenty-four dancers, was not differentiated. During rehearsals for *Town Topics* (1915), Wayburn toyed with using baseball positions to designate the various male chorus groups. However, the terms never became general currency, and he soon dropped the idea.

The divisions in the female chorus, by contrast, were both clearly defined and colorfully named. The categories, in ascending order of height, are given with their slang terms:

E's—5'–5'3", called "pony teams," "pacers" or "limies."

D's—5'–5'5", called "ponies" or "thoroughbreds."

C's—5'2"–5'6", called "chickens" or "squabs."

B's—5'5"–5'7", called "chickens" or "peaches."

A's—5'7" and up, called "show girls."[3]

Wayburn's male chorus seldom performed specialty work. Rather, it served primarily as a frame for the female soloist. It was usually placed in a line, semicircle, or inverted V, and typically performed in the space between the footlights or apron and the first light border—that is, in the shallowest area of the stage. The male chorus generally worked in musical comedy or tap technique, although in ballroom-derived acts, chorus members occasionally served as partners. In Wayburn's later shows, the male chorus was chiefly used to dress the stage. In "'Neath the South Sea Moon" from the 1922 edition of the *Follies*, for instance, he placed it behind the scene's two female choruses.

One male chorus specialty that Wayburn did employ, especially in the early 1910s, was the chair dance. A typical example of this was the number "Hello Cupid, Send Me A Fellow" in the musical *Broadway to Paris* (1912), where a chorus of sixteen men, dressed in top hats and tails, formed a frame behind the vocalist Marion Sunshine.[4] The number called for seventeen chairs, which were set in a very shallow semicircle across the front of the stage. Four moments from the dance survive in photographs. In one, the men stand facing left, each behind a chair, while Sunshine skips in front; in another, they stand, still in the same position, while she, now seated in the middle chair, sings into a prop telephone; in the third, all stand in front of their chairs; in the fourth, she dances in the center, while the men step from chair to chair behind.[5]

The chorus of E-dancers was always a precision team.[6] The category had its origin in the Original English Pony Ballet and reproduced the group's line formations. The typical E dance number was performed by six, eight, twelve, or sixteen short women in a straight line across the front of the stage. Frequently, the area behind the line was closed off by a curtain or screen.

E-dancers always worked in musical comedy technique. Their numbers frequently included the shadowing devices of tandem work. In a typical formation a line of sixteen faced the audience, each dancer kicking her right foot to the left while tilting her body to the right. Although Wayburn's choreography for E-dancers anticipated the precision style associated today with the Rockettes, the scale of their movements was very different. Kicks, for instance, seldom rose higher than fifty degrees. What gave the steps their impact was that they were performed by a large number of dancers simultaneously.

D-dancers, who were approximately the same height as E's, occasionally worked in precision choreography. Unlike E's, however, they also did individualized work. The precision numbers that Wayburn staged for "ponies" were generally performed on staircases or platforms. In "When Uncle Sam is the Ruler of the Waves," a section of the patriotic Act II finale of *The Century Girl* (1916), the D's worked on a double staircase set on the theater's revolve. "Sime" described the scene in detail in *Variety*:

> The revolving stage is employed. On it are high flights of stairs, and, with the background of [Joseph] Urban scenery, the set looks like a steeplechase course. Girls [A's or B's] in patriotic dress line the edge of the stage, in single file. Behind them are grouped sailors and soldiers, girls and boys [all female D's]. As the stage commences to revolve, the girls edging the stage do a single side step, to the music, while those behind, march and countermarch, in twos, fours and eights alternately, up and over and down the flights of stairs.[7]

Another type of number that Wayburn staged for D-choruses, especially in the *Ziegfeld Midnight Frolics*, was the flirtation dance. In these numbers, which employed musical comedy or tap technique, props were used as an audience-involving device. In the "Knitting Dance" from the December 1917 *Frolics*, for example, the men in the front row were asked by the dancers to hold their balls of wool as they knitted and sang "Every Girl is Doing Her Bit."[8] The flirtation number in the October 1919 *Frolics* opened with Frances White, who frequently led Wayburn's D-chorus numbers, hidden in a giant Easter egg covered with ribbons. As the dancers sang "pull 'em," they handed the ribbon ends to the men in the front row: the egg burst open, and White emerged to finish the song, "The Surprise Package." Among Wayburn's many other flirtation dances was "Every Girl is Fishing," a number that he used in the December 1916 *Frolics* and duplicated the following month in the Hippodrome revue *Zig-Zag*. In this number, D-dancers worked on glass-bottom ramps and dangled fishing lines to the audience seated below.

C and B groups were the least differentiated of Wayburn's choruses. In his largest revues, such as the 1919 *Frolics* and the 1922 *Follies*, the B-chorus worked only in musical comedy technique, while the C-chorus did acrobatics, ballet, and eccentric bucks (a form of tap work with kicks and poses sharply angled to the oblique). In smaller shows, however, the B- and C-choruses were merged.

Both these choruses did characterizational work. The "Egyptians" who framed Evan Burrows-Fontaine's Arabian number in *The Ed Wynn Carnival* (1920) were characterizational B's and C's, as were the "Hawaiians" who surrounded Ann Pennington, the Dolly Sisters, and Gilda Gray in their various hulas. Wayburn described his method for teaching such work in many promotional articles. In a 1913 issue of the *Green Book*, he described the following exercise:

> Thus…in a figure in which the chorus will be imitating a principal who is a silly ass Englishman, using a monocle, etc., the movements of the chorus with the monocle will all be based on counts of eight. Thus I can sit down, say "Monocle" and begin to count "One, two, three, four, etc." and each number will mean a different position of the monocle, first in the hand, then raised to the eye, then a squint, then drop the monocle, and so on. When a chorus is with a principal playing a French part, the work I have to give them is entirely different from what they would do with a German, an Italian, a Spaniard, an Englishman, a Chinese or a Mexican character.[9]

Framing work was the primary function of both C- and B-choruses. Although both were made up of skilled dancers, they were frequently employed in scenes in which primary effect was not choreographic. They were used, for example, in the many Wayburn-Ziegfeld scenes featuring black light and phosphorescent effects. Among these was the "Will O'The Wisp" number in the January 1916 *Frolics*, which used combined C- and B-choruses (totaling forty dancers) and a male vocalist, and two complementary scenes from the *Ziegfeld Follies of 1922*. The first, "It's Getting Dark on Broadway," was an eccentric buck performed by Gilda Gray and sixteen C-dancers. The second, "Laceland," employed a fully differentiated female chorus with the C-dancers working on pointe and the B's framing the A-chorus.

In the few nonframing scenes that Wayburn choreographed for C-choruses, the dancers worked in single or multiple line formations in back of the vocalists. Frequently, in these numbers, the dancers were treated as scenic elements. For instance, in "Tulip Time" from the *Ziegfeld Follies of 1919*, they were partially hidden behind rows of prop tulips.[10] Other dances that did not involve framing effects tended to be musical comedy or tap numbers set to songs that featured the word "chicken." Among these numbers were "The Chicken Rag" in *The Never Homes* (1911), "Everybody Loves a Chicken" from *Broadway to Paris* (1912), and "The Chicken Coop Rag," written for *Town Topics* (1915).

Of all the dance numbers staged by Wayburn, the best known involved the least movement. They were choreographed for the A-chorus, or "show girls," and their basic movement was the "Ziegfeld Walk." As reconstructed from interviews, demonstrations, photographs, and floor plans, the "Ziegfeld Walk" was a slow promenade down a staircase or a system of platforms at an oblique angle to the audience.[11] The footwork was simple—a step forward with the outside foot, followed by a closing step with the inside foot. The step forward took place on the first beat of a four-count measure, and the closing step on the third. Because of the physical limitations of the design (generally by Joseph Urban), the outside foot followed the line of the set. For example, a show girl walking down a stage right staircase would begin each walk with her right (outside) foot. The closing step was dictated by another element of Urban's design. As revealed by his floor plans for the *Ziegfeld Follies*, he frequently designed staircases with risers higher than the architectural standard of seven and one-half inches; indeed, even at this height, an A-dancer could not negotiate the treads without a closing step that enabled her to regain her balance.[12]

When performing the "Ziegfeld Walk," the dancer angled her body in the opposite direction from her movement path. Thus, if she were descending the stage right staircase, her torso faced downstage left. Her face was straight to the audience, and her arms were extended to the side, with the hands drooping from the wrists: costumes involving trains were frequently looped up and attached to a bracelet. The outside shoulder tilted away from the arms and was balanced by the hip in opposition. Conventional opposition could not be used since the step pattern denied equal movement to the inside leg.

The physical design of the New Amsterdam Roof Theater, where the late-night *Frolics* were staged, demanded certain modifications of the "Ziegfeld Walk." Because of the short staircase connecting the theater's upper and lower stages, the dancers worked primarily on the ramps built over the side edges of the audience area. They still used the uneven step pattern, but because of the ramps, they had to angle the movement even more to the side, so that it became a kind of serpentine side step. The movement recalled Wayburn's choreography in *The Passing Show of 1912*, where the harem girls entered on a ramp in the center of the theater, over the heads of the audience.

A-dancers performed three basic numbers—simple processionals, montage processionals, and elimination pictures. In the latter, they literally walked out of enlarged illustrations. The first scene to use the device was staged not by Wayburn (despite his claim to the contrary), but by Earl Carroll, then at the end of his tenure as Wayburn's protégé.[13] In the scene, which came at the end of *The Passing Show of 1912*, the dancers hid in life-sized reproductions of Cole Phillips covers for *Life Magazine*.[14] Perhaps because he resented Carroll's invention, or because of a genuine dislike of the genre, Wayburn seems to have been the only dance director of the 1910s and 1920s who did not stage elimination pictures.

Processionals, on the other hand, were a Wayburn trademark. He staged them for various editions of the *Ziegfeld Follies* and *Midnight Frol-*

"A-dancers" or show girls in costume for the Ziegfeld Follies of 1922.
Ned Wayburn, The Art of Stage Dancing *(1925), p. 186.*

ics, using the staircases and platforms designed by Joseph Urban. The simple processional was an uncomplicated form based on the fashion show. The link with fashion shows predated Wayburn's arrival at the *Follies:* indeed, it began when Ziegfeld hired the couturiere Lucile (Lady Duff-Gordon) to design the *Follies* costumes. Under her influence, Julian Mitchell, Wayburn's choreographic predecessor at the *Follies,* adopted the technique of having mannequins move slowly down a runway or staircase toward the audience, displaying their gowns. Lucile's tenure at the *Follies* overlapped with Wayburn's, as did that of many of her mannequins.

Scenes built around the simple processional were generally divided into four parts. There was usually a song, monologue, or exchange of dialogue introducing the theme and design motif. Next came a song alluding to the pulchritude of the dancers, such as "A Pretty Girl is Like a Melody," "Beautiful Girls," "The Beautiful Garden of Girls," or "You Don't Need the Wine to Have a Wonderful Time, When They Still Make Those Beautiful Girls." Then came the processional itself. The scene ended with a reprise of the song, as the dancers took their final poses on the staircase. Although the format was similar, the *Follies* processionals, because of the enormous New Amsterdam stage, tended to be longer and to involve more dancers than those choreographed for the *Frolics.*

The ingenuity that Wayburn, Ziegfeld, and the scriptwriters brought to the creation of these scenes was outstanding. They came up with a host of clever motifs: New York neighborhoods (January 1916 *Frolics*), America's allies and assorted flowers (*Follies of 1917*), popular Broadway plays and wedding anniversaries (December 1917 *Frolics*), cars (April 1918 *Frolics*), bridal trousseaux (*Follies of 1922*); and, as Prohibition went into effect, soft drinks (*Follies of 1919*).

One of the most inventive of Wayburn's simple processionals was the Jewels scene in the October 1919 *Frolics*. In this number, the dancers walked down the staircase in the order that their gems were mentioned in the accompanying song, "Beautiful Jewel." The first letter of each jewel—diamond, emerald, amethyst, ruby, (dark) emerald, sapphire, and topaz—spelled out the title of the song, "Dearest," which accompanied the descent of the final show girl, Dolores. This edition of the *Frolics* also included a processional with a bird motif: here, Dolores appeared as the White Peacock.

The complex processional, which recalled Wayburn's montage system, was used primarily in the *Follies*. In this genre, after descending the staircase or system of platforms, the dancers posed in a way that depicted some aspect of the theme. For example, in "A Pretty Girl is Like a Melody" from the 1919 *Follies* (probably the song most often associated with the A-chorus), each of the dancers "personified" a melody sung by the tenor John Steele. The musical selections, which came from the repertory of popular classics, included Offenbach's "Barcarole" (from his *Tales of Hoffmann*) and Mendelssohn's "Spring Song." The Mendelssohn piece was associated in this period with Gertrude Hoffmann's imitations of Maud Allan, but it is unclear whether the action alluded to this.

When Wayburn staged scenes for a full chorus, he generally emphasized the differences among the groups. In "Bring on the Girls" from the 1922 *Follies*, he used all five chorus groups and five of his dance techniques—musical comedy, tap, ballet, acrobatics (called "sure-fire dances of today" in the program), and processionals. In "Laceland," which he choreographed for the same show, he worked with three chorus groups simultaneously. Apart from the soloists (a female vocalist and two romantic "ballerinas," one costumed as a butterfly), there were twenty-four dancers onstage at the climax of the scene.[15] The chorus, which did not include E's or D's, performed various numbers, such as "The Dutch Vision," where four B's represented lace makers, and "The Ballet of Motives," danced by twelve C's. Two of the eight A's, the Connor Twins, played pages, while the remaining six were given individualized parts, as in a simple processional.

Dancers who played named parts nearly always belonged to the A-chorus. In "Laceland," each item of the bridal trousseau—Fan, Gown, Lace Stockings, Parasol, Handkerchief, Veil—was personified by an A. In the final tableau the soloists posed at the center stage. In front, framing the ballet soloist, was the C-chorus, arranged in a double semicircle. On the next highest level of platforms were the eight A's, with the Connor Twins facing each other (their specialty was tandem mirroring work), holding the train of the Gown's costume; the other A's faced the audience.

Dolores as the White Peacock, Ziegfeld Midnight Frolics, *1919. Robinson Locke Scrapbook, Billy Rose Theater Collection, New York Public Library for the Performing Arts.*

Finally, on the top platform, framing the butterfly soloist, were the lace maker B's.

Despite the popularity of individual performers, the success of Wayburn's musical numbers ultimately depended on the chorus. Its formations defined the stage space, directed attention to the soloists, and created visually arresting stage pictures. Wayburn's use of the specialty chorus had an enormous influence on the development of American dance technique in general and on the Broadway stage in particular. By eliminating the need for dancers to be adept in every idiom, he created a generation of highly skilled "specialist" performers—and put them in the chorus.

Conclusion

As we have seen, Ned Wayburn's chief innovations as a dance director lay in the broad range of technical vocabularies that he routinely employed, his revamping of the divisions within the female chorus and increasingly "specialized" choreography for each of its groups, and the concept of performance hierarchy that governed his manipulation of soloists and masses. His ability to adapt his work to the needs of various theatrical forms made him one of the most sought-out—and influential—dance directors of his time.

The two media most strongly affected by Wayburn's work were film and the musical stage. A third, television, might well have profited from his influence, had he not died just as the medium was beginning to develop as a commercial enterprise. Wayburn's influence on live performance was greatest during his years on Broadway—that is, during the first two decades or so of the twentieth century. Subsequently it continued through the Prologs that he continued to choreograph into the 1930s. His influence on film musicals was greatest in the period of transition between the silent and sound era.

Although Wayburn's innovations as a dance director left a deep imprint on twentieth-century live performance, their impact on Broadway itself was limited. By the mid-1920s, the scale of Broadway shows was contracting, both for economic reasons and because of the growing popularity of "little shows." Music, too, was changing, and the ABA form that was the basis of Wayburn's routines was partly discarded. Wayburn's innovations were chiefly adopted by Prolog choreographers, rather than by his successors on Broadway.

Prolog choreographers adopted not only his major dance idioms, but also his combination vocabularies and unconventional single techniques, such as toe tapping, precision acrobatics, and toe and tap adagio work, all of which they popularized. Since these choreographers, who included Chester Hale at New York's Capitol Theater, Leon Leonidoff at the Roxy Theater and Radio City Music Hall, Larry Ceballos, and Fanchon and Marco in Los Angeles, had to mount a new show every week, Wayburn's stock of techniques proved very useful.

Prologs also carried on Wayburn's use of the chorus as a framing device and some of his methods for integrating specialties. From 1924 to 1936 each Fanchon and Marco West Coast Prolog employed a precision chorus, known as "The Sunkist Beauties," that worked in tap, musical comedy, or toe tapping technique. Like revues and other musical genres, Prologs also featured individual specialty acts—vocalists, dancers, monologuists, and social dance or adagio teams—that were incorporated in var-

ious ways into the whole. The resemblance between the West Coast Prologs and Wayburn's feature acts and montages is obvious.

East Coast Prologs, which were bigger in scale and toured a circuit of
larger theaters, also included differentiated choruses that followed the
model of Wayburn's. Many of Chester Hale's Prologs for the Capitol
Theater, for instance, employed a precision tap team, a precision toe tapping group, a conventional musical comedy chorus, and a corps de ballet.
As late as the 1970s the stage shows at the Radio City Music Hall used
precision choruses that maintained the same basic divisions as Wayburn's.

Wayburn's influence on motion picture choreography did not stem
directly from his own film work. *Potash and Perlmutter* (1923) was treated as a comedy, and most critics ignored Evelyn Law's interpolated dance,
while *The Great White Way* (1924), a star-studded extravaganza, seems to
have been a failure. Once again, his influence was exerted through Prologs. Many of the late silent and early sound musicals adopted the format
of a Wayburn revue: they featured differentiated choruses, a range of technical vocabularies, interpolated specialties, and dancers of various physical
and performance types. *The King of Jazz* (1930), a musical revue built
around Paul Whiteman and his orchestra, had a typical Wayburn finale:
lines of dancers moved toward the camera, displaying, by turn, his specialized techniques. The title of the number was "The Melting Pot."

The use of formations completely visible only from above, considered
one of the most innovative aspects of early sound film choreography, also
derived from Wayburn. Although there is no evidence that Busby Berkeley ever worked directly with him, there are documented links between
Wayburn and other dance directors in films who used the device, including Bobby Connolly, Albertina Rasch, Pearl Eaton, and John Lonergan.
The creation of shapes that changed dramatically when viewed from
skewed or raised angles was a device that Wayburn frequently used in
revues, including shows in which both Eaton and Connolly appeared.

Wayburn's influence may be judged as well from the exceptionally
high caliber of his artistic collaborators. By this standard, his influence
was immense. Among the songwriters he hired were Harold Atteridge,
Gene Buck, Irving Caesar, Anne Caldwell, Earl Carroll, Bob Cole, Ana-
tole Friedland, Victor Herbert, Gertrude Hoffmann, Max Hoffmann,
Dorothy Jardon, J. Rosamond Johnson, Jerome Kern, Paul Lannin,
Blanche Merrill, Sigmund Romberg, Jean Schwartz, Dave Stamper, and
Vincent Youmans. He gave very early jobs to the Gershwin brothers,
although, interestingly, he did not hire them as a team. Instead, he paired
George Gershwin with Irving Caesar ("Swanee" was one of the results),
and Ira Gershwin, then writing as "Arthur Francis," with Vincent
Youmans (in *Two Little Girls in Blue*).

Wayburn's own assistants, including Arthur Evans and John Lonergan,
did not go on to prolific careers as dance directors. However, many of his
dancers and other collaborators did. These included Earl Carroll, Pearl
Eaton, Gertrude Hoffmann, Harry Pilcer, Albertina Vitak, and George

White. Among the performers who either worked or trained with him, many became stars in vaudeville, theater, film, radio, and television—Adele and Fred Astaire, Gilda Gray, Marilyn Miller, Ann Pennington, Barbara Stanwyck (under the name Ruby Stevens), Clifton Webb, and Mae West.

Wayburn was thus a major influence on performers just as he was on choreography, not only during his career but also long after it. Immensely prolific, he lived at a significant time in the development of the American musical theater. But he was also a unique figure in his own right, a dance director who extended both the boundaries of his art and its expression as popular entertainment.

Notes

Preface

1. For a discussion of structuralism and its implications for performance, see Michael Kirby's essay "Structural Analysis/Structural Theory" (*The Drama Review*, 20, No. 4 [Dec. 1976], pp. 52–68), and his book *The Art of Time: Essays on the Avant-Garde* (New York: Dutton, 1969).

Early Life and Influences

1. Samuel Fletcher Weyburn, *Weyburn-Wyborn Genealogy* (New York: Frank Allaben Genealogical Press, 1911), pp. 71, 90–91. Patents, stock certificates, letterheads, and advertisements for Weyburn manufacturing firms are in Scrapbooks 21,049, 21,053, and 21,070, Ned Wayburn Collection, Billy Rose Theater Collection, New York Public Library for the Performing Arts. As the scrapbooks assembled and donated by Mrs. Marguerite Kirby Wayburn in the Ned Wayburn Collection are not arranged in chronological order, they will be identified by accession number (21,049–21,070) rather than volume number. All further references to the Billy Rose Theater Collection will be denoted by the abbreviation BRTC.
2. Interview with Edward Claudius Weyburn, Jr., New York, 29 Nov. 1979.
3. *Weyburn-Wyborn Genealogy*, p. 99.
4. H.M.H., "Ned Wayburn," Unidentified Chicago-area newspaper, ca. 1904 (Ned Wayburn Scrapbook 21,061, BRTC). The reason for the adoption of the name "Rossiter" is a mystery to Edward Claudius Weyburn, Jr., although the above article claimed that it was Wayburn's middle name.
5. Advertisement for the Lyceum Theater, Chicago, *The Chicago Amusement News*, 8 Jan. 1893.
6. Ned Wayburn, *The Art of Stage Dancing* (New York: Ned Wayburn Studios of Stage Dancing, 1925), p. 25. All further references to this book will be to the 1925 edition.
7. *The Spirit of the Times*, 10 Oct. 1896 (Hart Conway Scrapbook, Robinson Locke Collection, BRTC).
8. Hart Conway, letter to Colonel John Hopkins, Chicago, [1896] (Ned Wayburn Scrapbook 21,049, BRTC).
9. "Faculty and Branches of Instruction," *The Yearbook of the Chicago Musical College*, 1895, 1896, 1898, 1900. Courtesy of the Newberry Library.
10. Announcement, Hart Conway School of Acting, [1896] (Ned Wayburn Scrapbook 21,049, BRTC).
11. Information on Jacobsen provided by Diana Haskell, curator of Modern Manuscripts, the Newberry Library; information on the immigration of Danish ballet masters to America provided in interview with Harold Christensen, San Anselmo, California, 30 Dec. 1976.
12. Albert Johanssen, *The House of Beadle and Adams*, 2 (Norman, Okla.: University of Oklahoma Press, 1950), pp. 22–24; [E.L. Pearson], "The Beadle

Collection," *The Bulletin of The New York Public Library*, 26, no. 27 (July 1922), pp. 550–629; T.H. Monstery, *El Rubio Bravo: King of the Swordsmen* (New York: Beadle and Adams, 1881).

13. "Ned Wayburn's Health and Beauty Course," p. 3B (Evelyn Law Scrapbook, BRTC).

14. For the relationship between Delsarte and MacKaye, see Rayda Walker Dillport, "The Pupils of François Delsarte" (M.A. thesis, Louisiana State University, 1946); and Virginia Elizabeth Morris, "The Influence of Delsarte in America as Revealed through the Lectures of Steele MacKaye" (M.A. thesis, Louisiana State University, 1941).

15. Steele MacKaye to Ida Simpson-Serven, New York, 3 Nov. 1883, MacKaye Family Papers, Special Collections, Baker Library, Dartmouth College. Simpson-Serven used this recommendation in her advertisement in the *Delsarte Recitation Book*, edited by Elsie Wilfor (1893).

16. Information provided by Eleanor M. Gehres, Western History Department, Denver Public Library.

17. Ida Simpson-Serven, "Harmonic Gymnastics," MacKaye Family Papers, Special Collections, Baker Library, Dartmouth College.

18. *Ibid.*, exercise no. 7.

19. F.C. Schrang, "Mysteries of the Chorus," *New York Tribune*, 7 May 1916 (Ned Wayburn Scrapbook 21,064, BRTC).

20. Wayburn, *The Art of Stage Dancing*, pp. 90–91.

21. Interview with Edward Claudius Weyburn, Jr., New York, 19 Nov. 1979.

22. C.H. Cleveland, Jr., *Dancing at Home and Abroad* (Boston: Oliver Ditson and Co., 1878), pp. 27–31.

23. *Ibid.*, p. 31.

24. Allan Dodworth, *Dancing and its Relation to Education and Social Life* (New York: Harper, 1905), pp. 157–302. H. Layton Walker, publisher of the *Two-Step Magazine*, included over 700 cotillion figures in his *Twentieth Century Cotillion Figures* (Buffalo, N.Y.: Two-Step Publishing Co., 1912).

25. Samuel Baron, *Complete Instructor in All the Society Dances of America* (New York: M. Young Publishers, 1881), pp. 22–23.

26. F. Leslie Clendenen, *Quadrille Book* (Chicago: Chart Music Publishing House, 1899), pp. 12–41.

27. Elizabeth Avis Middleton, *Scarf Fantastics* (New York: Edgar S. Werner Publishing and Supply Co., 1896). Edgar S. Werner was the leading publisher of Delsarte material in America.

28. Marguerite W. Morton, *Ideal Drills* (Philadelphia: Penn Publishing Co., 1926), n.p.; *Fancy Drills for Evening and Other Entertainments* (New York: Butterick Publishing Co., 1894), n.p.

29. Morton, *Ideal Drills*.

30. Program, State Street Theater, Chicago, n.d. (Ned Wayburn Scrapbook 21,049, BRTC).

31. A "coon-shouter" was a singer who specialized in blues songs between about 1895 and 1920. Male "coon-shouters" frequently worked in blackface, but Irwin, like most females, did not.

32. Free dance schools were sponsored by theater owners and managers to provide trained dancers for their shows. Wayburn arranged to use dancers from the Klaw and Erlanger school in his feature acts.

33. Herbert Gresham, an English actor, best known as a member of Augustin

Daly's theater company, was a director who specialized in staging the dialogue portions of pantomimes and spectacles in the first two decades of the twentieth century. Ernest d'Auban, a member of the famous family that had provided ballet masters to Covent Garden, the Kiralfy Brothers, and American spectacle producers, was best known for aerial ballets that combined classical technique with trapeze and ring work.

34. Barbara Naomi Cohen, "Chain Prologs: Dance at the Picture Palaces," *Dance Scope* (Fall 1978), p. 29.

35. Interview with Fred Astaire, Los Angeles, 5 Dec. 1979.

Dance Idioms and Performance Hierarchies

1. Wayburn, *The Art of Stage Dancing*, pp. 84–85.

2. George Lederer, untitled unpublished memoirs, 1927, p. 7 (George Lederer Clipping File, BRTC).

3. It should be noted that most of the dance numbers performed by the Original English Pony Ballet in the United States were not choreographed by Wayburn, Tiller, or George Lederer, but by a company member, Dorothy Marlowe, according to information in undated, unidentified newspapers in the Elizabeth, Louise, and Margaret Hawman, Beatrice Liddell, and Seppie McNeil unmounted clippings, Robinson Locke Collection, BRTC.

4. Wayburn, *The Art of Stage Dancing*, pp. 58, 97.

5. *Ibid.*, pp. 98–102.

6. Advertisement for Ned Wayburn's Home-Study Course in Stage Dancing, ca. 1925 (Ned Wayburn Institute for Dancing, Singing and Dramatics, Inc., unmounted clipping file, BRTC).

7. Wayburn, *The Art of Stage Dancing*, p. 121.

8. *Ibid.*

9. My "Modern Americanized Ballet: 'Her Stage of Perpetual Chiffon'" (*Dance Scope* [Summer 1980]), includes a technical comparison of Wayburn's ballet vocabulary and that of European ballet masters teaching in the United States between 1920 and 1925.

10. The speed of teaching was probably due to the frequency of classes (two hour-and-a-half lessons per day, five days a week), the intensity of teaching, and the fact that each dancer had to have had a two-month course in Ling gymnastics (called the Foundation Course) before beginning ballet. Ballet students were also expected to take private lessons and to study another form of dance concurrently.

Vaudeville Feature Acts

1. Daily column by "Chicot," Central News and Press Exchange, New York, 26 July 1903 (Epes Winthrop Sargent Scrapbook, BRTC).

2. "The Summer Theatre," *The Theatre Magazine* (July 1904), p. 160.

3. Program, New York Theater Roof, New York, week beginning 13 June 1904 (BRTC).

4. In all of Wayburn's early commissioned acts, and many of those presented by the Headline Vaudeville Production Company, female soloists did not change costumes for individual scenes, but, instead, remained in one outfit during the entire act. "Combination" is a technical costume term denoting

tights and bodices attached in a one-piece garment.

5. Wayburn retained title to the Headline Vaudeville Production Company until 1936. *Town Topics*, *The Demi-Tasse Revue*, and the Ben Ali Haggin Prologs were also produced under its aegis.

6. Clipping and half-tone reproductions of uncredited photographs in unidentified newspaper, ca. 1908 (Ned Wayburn unmounted clippings, BRTC); quotations from a review attributed to "Sime" (originally published in *Variety*, 7 Aug. 1907) in promotional articles published in *The Pittsburgh Leader*, 5 Jan. 1908 (Hilarion and Rosalia Ceballos Scrapbook, Robinson Locke Collection, BRTC).

7. *Variety*, 22 Sept. 1906 (Ned Wayburn Scrapbook 21,058, BRTC).

8. Max Hoffmann, like Wayburn, had been a performing pianist whose specialty was ragtime arrangements of familiar classics and popular songs.

9. Caption of half-tone reproduction of photograph, *The Standard* (New York), 1 July 1901 (Eleanor Falk unmounted clippings, Robinson Locke Collection, BRTC).

10. Caption of half-tone reproduction of uncredited photograph in unidentified New York-area newspaper, 2 July 1901 (Eleanor Falk Un-mounted clippings, Robinson Locke Collection BRTC).

11. Half-tone reproduction of uncredited photograph in unidentified New York-area newspaper, ca. 1902 (Chorus: U.S. Scrapbook, BRTC).

12. Specifications for Color Registration for the years 1903 to 1905, Archives of the Jockey Club, New York, and the New York State Racing Authority. "Colors" is a legal term denoting the hues and patterns used on a jockey's uniform. Wayburn used the "colors" as a theatrical device in *The Futurity Winner* (1906), in which the dénouement depended on the audience's recognition of a jockey whose face was hidden: the program helpfully printed "colors" for the jockeys.

13. *The Brooklyn Citizen*, 12 July 1906 (Ned Wayburn Scrapbook 21,057, BRTC). All these props were typical of Original English Pony Ballet dances.

14. Social dances of this period, especially the hesitations and early one-steps, were performed with men and women each taking steps of the same size; because of the narrow skirts, the steps were no longer than one-and-a-half feet.

15. Untitled article in *The Theatre Magazine* (Summer 1903), p. 123.

16. *Ibid.*

17. "Ned Wayburn talks about his Minstrel Misses," reprinted in the souvenir program distributed at Keith's Theater, Boston, week beginning 14 Sept. 1903 (Harvard Theater Collection).

18. Program, New York Theater Roof, week beginning 13 June 1904, Harvard Theater Collection.

19. The only illustration is a cartoon by "Harry Harmony" that shows the dancer applying blackface, while wearing the Daisy costume used four scenes earlier.

20. Unidentified newspaper, Albany, N.Y., 28 May 1906; *New York Dramatic Mirror*, 9 June 1906 (Ned Wayburn Scrapbook 21,057, BRTC).

21. In the prologue to the act, members of the chorus were not dressed identically, but each performer still had a total of five costume changes.

22. Half-tone reproduction of uncredited photograph in unidentified New York-area periodical (possibly *The Green Book Album*) (Ned Wayburn

Scrapbook 21,070, BRTC).

23. Wayburn, *The Art of Stage Dancing*, p. 34.

24. Copies of correspondence using this letterhead can be found in Ned Wayburn Scrapbooks, 21,049, 21,054, 21,068 and 21,070, BRTC.

25. The running order was changed during the fall 1906 tour.

26. Jerome H. Remick and Company published the song as "Fandango Fannie" in 1907.

27. *The Baltimore American*, 25 Sept. 1906 (Ned Wayburn Scrapbook 21,058, BRTC).

28. Wayburn, *The Art of Stage Dancing*, p. 267.

29. *The Sun and the Globe* (New York), 22 Feb. 1903, Sec. 2, p. 6.

30. *The Troy Press* (Troy, N.Y.), 22 May 1906 (Ned Wayburn Scrapbook 21,057, BRTC).

31. *Ibid.*

32. As in Wayburn's commissioned feature acts, the soloists remained in one outfit throughout.

33. Genevieve Stebbins, *Society Gymnastics and Voice Culture* (New York: Edgar S. Werner Publishing and Supply Co., 1888), p. 128. This may also have been a stock vaudeville gesture.

34. *New York Daily News*, 28 July 1906 (Ned Wayburn Scrapbook 21,057, BRTC).

35. *The Troy Press, op. cit.*

36. For reviews, see Ned Wayburn unmounted clippings, Robinson Locke Collection, BRTC, and Ned Wayburn Scrapbooks 21,057, 21,058 and 21,060, BRTC.

37. *Fancy Drills for Evening and Other Entertainments*, p. 35, and illustration printed on inside front and back covers.

38. *Variety*, 2 June 1906 (Ned Wayburn Scrapbook 21,061, BRTC).

39. *The Troy Press, op. cit.*

40. *Cincinnati Star*, 20 Oct. 1906 (Ned Wayburn Scrapbook 21,061, BRTC).

41. Earl Carroll, "Making a Song Hit," *The Music Trades* (9 Dec. 1911), n.p. (Ned Wayburn Scrapbook 21,050, BRTC).

42. *Variety*, 22 Sept. 1906 (Ned Wayburn Scrapbook 21,058, BRTC).

43. *The Troy Press, op. cit.*

44. *New York Daily News*, 28 July 1906 (Ned Wayburn Scrapbook 21,058, BRTC).

45. *Ibid.*

46. *Cincinnati Star, op. cit.*

47. Verse 1, line 5.

48. *Cincinnati Star, op. cit.*

Individual Specialty Acts

1. Carroll, "Making a Song Hit."

2. The onstage "audience" consisted of supernumeraries, the characters in the musical comedy itself, and wax dummies representing New York first-nighters and critics, such as "Diamond" Jim Brady and Alan Dale. Promotional article, *The New York Telegraph*, 20 May 1909 (Blanche Ring Scrapbook, Robinson Locke Collection, BRTC). Wayburn's partial script for *The Midnight Sons* is in the collection of scripts and skits given by Wayburn to

radio and film comedian Ole Olsen (Ole Olsen Papers, University of Southern California).

3. Promotional articles in unnamed newspapers, 1908–1914 (Mazie King and Gladys Moore unmounted clipping files, Robinson Locke Collection, BRTC).

4. American imitations and parodies of Anna Pavlova tended to be inaccurate when portraying her male partners. In many parodies, for instance, she was depicted as performing with Vaslav Nijinsky, with whom she seldom danced in Europe and never in the United States.

5. Verse 1, lines 1–8, refrain, line 1, "The Bacchanale Rag."

6. The size of the *Les Sylphides* chorus in the *Follies* is uncertain. Even though the Ballets Russes performed the Fokine work in New York with its usual complement of dancers (i.e., one male soloist, several female soloists, and a corps of sixteen women), American audiences were more accustomed to Theodore Kosloff's production (for Gertrude Hoffmann's Saison des Ballets Russes, 1910–1912), which used twenty-two corps dancers, four female soloists, and four men.

7. Program, New Amsterdam Theater, 12 June 1916. Although no orchestration for this scene can be located, it is likely that the musical arrangers integrated themes from the various ballets with instrumental cues for some of the comics, notably Brice, Hardy, and Williams.

8. The script may also have included references to Nijinsky's marriage and subsequent quarrel with Diaghilev, his relationship to Pavlova, and the disappointment voiced by many New York critics about the Ballets Russes repertory. For the reception of the Ballets Russes in America, see Nesta Macdonald, *Diaghilev Observed* (New York: Dance Horizons, 1975), pp. 136–213; for additional information on satires of Pavlova, Nijinsky, and Mordkin, see Barbara Naomi Cohen, "Ballet Satire in the Early Broadway Revue," *Dance Scope* (Winter-Spring 1979), pp. 44–50, and "Waldorf Dryginsky and the Little American Girl," *Dance Data* (Fall-Winter 1981), which includes an anthology of satirical songs by Harold Atteridge, Gene Buck, Louis Hirsch, Blanche Merrill, and Dave Stamper.

9. Verse 1, lines 2–6, refrain, lines 5–9. "Cushka" (Verse 1, line 5), which Harold Wentworth's *Dictionary of American Slang* (New York: Crowell, 1960) defines as "Money; especially profit, bribe or spending money," refers to the huge sums paid to Nijinsky to perform.

10. *The New York Times*, 13 June 1913 (Ned Wayburn Scrapbook 21,054, BRTC).

11. Program, Century Theater, New York, various dates during the 1916 and 1917 Ballets Russes seasons in New York (Personal Collection, and Dyagilev Ballets Russes Reserve Clipping and Program files, Dance Collection, New York Public Library for the Performing Arts).

12. The scenarios in which Wayburn proposed the set concept, dated 6 May 1913, preceded the "OK'd" script of 31 May 1913, and the working script of 13 June 1913. In the first two documents, the set was assigned to the Act II finale (Scene 5). All documents in Harold Attridge, Misc. Script Scrapbook, BRTC. My description of *The Allegory* is based on clipping file material, BRTC. A full analysis of this and MacKaye's other suffragist pageants can be found in Karen J. Blair's "Pageantry for Women's Rights: The Career of Hazel MacKaye, 1913–1923," *Theatre Survey*, 31, No. 1 (May 1990).

13. The standard riser of seven-and-one-half inches (with treads measuring eight-and-one-half inches) would produce a staircase that was twenty-one feet three inches high and reaching approximately twenty-four feet one inch back on the stage. This could be effectively masked by the Winter Garden's twenty-nine-foot proscenium even without a tormentor curtain.

14. Program, Winter Garden Theater, 25 July 1913; reviews from New York-area newspapers, 25 July 1913 (Ned Wayburn Scrapbooks 21,054 and 21,070, BRTC).

15. Mrs. Pankhurst was the founder of the Women's Social and Political Union. George Monroe worked with the Lew Fields company; his cook was among the well-known personalities depicted in the onstage audience of the Merri Murray Variety Theater.

16. Scores for the First Violin, Flute, and Trombone, 86 (6), Shubert Archive.

17. *New York Herald*, 25 July 1913; *The New York Times*, 25 July 1913 (Ned Wayburn Scrapbook 21,054, BRTC).

18. The pendulum step also appeared in work that did not involve pointe, such as the musical comedy routine from the 1926 from the Dance Masters of America Annual Normal Course and Convention, Step 4, measures 5–8.

19. The Vienna stair dance may have been staged by Vincenzo Romeo, an Italian ballet master working at the Vienna State Opera. According to a salary list (ca. July 1913) for *Passing Show of 1913*, Romeo was on the show's payroll, although receiving no credit in the program.

20. Beginning with the 2,700 steps of the Metropolitan Tower, New York, Mazie King claimed to have hopped on pointe down the stairs of buildings in Chicago, Denver, and San Francisco. See promotional articles in the *New York Mirror*, 26 Apr. 1911, and the *San Francisco Call*, 12 May 1914 (Mazie King unmounted clipping file, Robinson Locke Collection, BRTC).

21. Act I finale script, entitled "The Capitol Steps" 86(6). In 1913, there was a New York sheriff named Julius Harberger.

22. The genre, known as "Becky Songs," was popular between 1910 and 1923. Like "Sadie Songs," they were associated with Fanny Brice and written by, among others, Irving Berlin and Blanche Merrill. Among the songs in this genre were "Becky from Babylon" and "Becky is Back in the Ballet."

23. *Boston Traveller-Herald*, 27 Oct. 1913 (Swan Wood unmounted clipping file, Robinson Locke Collection, BRTC). A similar statement was made by Wood in the *New York Review*, 5 Aug. 1913.

24. Verse 1, lines 3–8, refrain, lines 1–4, "The Golden Stairs of Love."

25. *The Dictionary of American Slang* (1960) defines "tangle-footed" as "drunk on cheap whiskey"; *The Random House Dictionary of the English Language* (1976) defines "monkey wrench" as "something that interferes with functioning."

26. *New York Telegraph*, 7 Jan. 1917 (Fred Nice, Jr. unmounted clipping file, Robinson Locke Collection, BRTC).

27. Script, "The Capitol Steps."

28. Scores for First Violin (i.e. Concertmaster), Flute, Trombone, and Harp, 86 (6), Shubert Archive.

29. White Studio key sheets, vol. 16, 538, p. 20, nos. 24, 26, and 28, BRTC.

30 Information and programs courtesy of Daniel Friedmann, Theatre Museum, London.

31. *New York Morning Telegraph*, 4 Oct. 1913 (Ned Wayburn Scrapbook

21,055, BRTC).

32. Half-tone reproductions of uncredited photographs originally published in *The Sketch* (London), 8 Oct. 1913 (Ned Wayburn Scrapbook 21,055, BRTC).

33. *The Graphic*, 11 Oct. 1913.

34. Program, Broadway Theater, New York, 22 May 1909.

35. Photographs of this pose appeared in promotional materials, newspapers, and on the covers of published sheet music for "Come and Dance with Me," "The Gaby Glide," and "When Gaby Did the Gaby Glide." The White Studio negative for the photograph on the sheet music cover is not extant, but a contact (or key) sheet copy is bound with shots from *The Honeymoon Express*.

36. Half-tone reproduction of uncredited photographs, *The Boston Traveller*, 5 Nov. 1921 (Evelyn Law Scrapbook, BRTC).

37. The ballet references appeared between 1909 and 1925; the *kazachok* ones usually date from the publicity anticipating the 1922 tour of the Chauve-Souris.

38. *The Atlanta Georgian*, 10 Aug. 1912 (Adelaide and Hughes Scrapbook, BRTC).

39. Refrain, "The Gertrude Hoffmann Glide." Hoffmann's imitations of Maud Allan's *Salomé* and *Spring Song* date from 1908; the reference to "Russians" alludes to her Saison des Ballets Russes. Imitations of Cohan and Tanguay were part of Hoffmann's "Borrowed Art" act, as were her "reviews" of Ethel Barrymore, Isadora Duncan, Eddie Foy, Harry Lauder, Ruth St. Denis, and others.

40. Interview with Deslys in unidentified New York-area newspaper, ca. Apr. 1913 (Harry Pilcer Scrapbook, Robinson Locke Collection, BRTC).

41. Gladys Crozier, *The Tango and How To Do It* (London: Andrew Melrose, 1913), p. 46. This tango was named for Maurice Mouvet, who, with Florence Walton, formed one of America's best known and most influential exhibition ballroom teams. Their greatest impact on theatrical choreography was made through the introduction of the apache dance.

42. Apr. 1913, interview, *op. cit.* A song of that name was interpolated by Blanche Ring into *The Wall Street Girl* (1912). Deslys may have meant to refer to that song, to the song performed by Al Jolson in *Vera Violette* called "Rum-tum-tiddle," or to a different song. She may, of course, have used the phrase to refer to a song whose title she had forgotten.

43. Unpaginated sides, *The Honeymoon Express*, 8 Oct. 1913, Shubert Archive.

44. Reviews of *The Honeymoon Express* in New York-area newspapers, 7 Feb. 1913 (Ned Wayburn Scrapbook 21,053, BRTC).

45. *The Atlanta Georgian*, 10 Aug. 1912; Crozier, *The Tango*, p. 125.

46. *The World*, New York, 25 July 1909 (Rosalia and Hilarion Ceballos Scrapbook, Robinson Locke Collection, BRTC).

47. *The New York Globe and Commercial Advertiser*, 18 June 1918. Heywood Broun in the *New York Tribune* (18 June 1918) stated that the effect was broken at the end of the scene when all four performers took curtain calls (Ned Wayburn Scrapbook 21,067, BRTC).

48. Information compiled from New York-area and out-of-town reviews in Oscar Shaw Scrapbook, Evelyn Law Scrapbook, and Ned Wayburn Scrapbook 21,054, BRTC.

49. Richard L. Stokes, *St. Louis Post*, 13 Feb. 1922 (Jack Donahue Scrapbook, BRTC).

50. There was also a subgenre of "Sadie" and Arabian songs that outlived the genre's original popularity. Typical of this song type, which was prompted by Prohibition, was Harold Atteridge and Sigmund Romberg's "Sahara—Soon We'll Be Dry Like You" from the Al Jolson vehicle, *Monte Christo, Jr.* Anti-Prohibition satires in scripts and lyrics predated the actual enforcement date of the Eighteenth Amendment, which went into effect between 1 July 1919 and 20 January 1920.

51. Interview with Florence O'Denishawn, New York, 25 Jan. 1979.

52. *New York Tribune*, 4 May 1921 (Evelyn Law Scrapbook, BRTC).

53. Jack Donahue, "Hoofing," *The Saturday Evening Post*, 14 Sept. 1929, p. 237.

54. Prof. A. Peters, *Des Leçons de Danse: le Shimmy et la Java* (Paris: Editions Nilsson, 1920), Pt. 1.

55. Albert and Josephine Butler, *Encyclopedia of Social Dance*, 1976 ed., unpaginated entry for the Shimmy.

56. Peters, *Des Leçons de Danse*.

57. Refrain 1, lines 8–9, "When They're Old Enough to Know Better, It's Better to Leave Them Alone." The placement of the word "shimmy" should be noted: the device of placing the punned word in the same place in each line of the couplet was typical of songs written for Cantor.

58. [G. Hepburn Wilson], "Dances and Music of Hawaii," *The Modern Dance Magazine*, Nov. 1916, pps. 10–11, 17, 20.

59. Although most of these books were similar to those by Frederick O'Brien (which Gilda Gray claimed had inspired her hula), some were anthologies of genuine Hawaiian music and dances. This category included Nathaniel B. Emerson's *Unwritten Literature of Hawaii* (originally written for the Bureau of American Ethnology), which Wayburn could have consulted. Again, however, the notion of accuracy in these dances is irrelevant.

60. In the design scheme of the 1916 *Follies*, Urban set a frame around each scene, placing the frames back on the stage; in the 1922 *Follies*, he built a realistic grass shack, through which Gray made her entrance.

61. "Gilda Gray's South Sea Dance," *Dance Lovers Magazine*, Oct. 1924, p. 12.

Chorus Specialty Acts

1. The onstage pool was a reference to Otis Skinner's recent production of *Kismet*.

2. This had an obvious influence on film staging. The link between Wayburn and early sound film dance directors is discussed in the conclusion.

3. These were the heights in 1913; by 1923, the tallest height in each category had risen by an average of 1.5 inches. See Mary Morgan, "Handling Humanity in Masses," *The Theatre Magazine*, Feb. 1913, pp. 178–179; and George Vaux Bacon, "Chorus Girls in the Making," *Green Book*, Oct. 1913, pp. 575–576.

4. K.M., "Remaking a Musical Show," *The Boston Evening Transcript*, 12 Oct. 1912 (Ned Wayburn Scrapbook 21,053, BRTC).

5. R.H. Burnside, the dance director of many Winter Garden musicals, used chair dances as preludes to social dance-derived numbers. It is not known why Wayburn rejected this convention.

6. Bacon, "Chorus Girls in the Making," p. 577.

7. *Variety*, 10 Nov. 1916; Wayburn also used the combination of precision dancers and staircases in the Act I finale of *Miss 1917*, in which the chorus played dolls.

8. *New York Evening Sun*, 31 Dec. 1917 (Ned Wayburn Scrapbook 21,055, BRTC). Knitting was considered to be a patriotic duty for women during the war, and was encouraged by knitting drives sponsored by the Red Cross.

9. Bacon, "Chorus Girls in the Making," pp. 577–578.

10. "Tulip Time" is a classic example of a song in which all the topical or descriptive references were placed at noncritical points in the rhyme scheme. Although the title of the song and elements of the set refer to Holland, the lyrics make little mention of that country. There is no reason to believe that the choreography for the number used traditional Dutch clog dancing.

11. Interviews with Doris Vinton, New York, 20 Oct. 1978; Carone Paynter, Los Angeles, 7 Dec. 1978; and Florence O'Denishawn, New York, 8 Jan. 1979. It should be noted that in one number the dancers walked *up* rather than down the staircase. This number, which was designed by Erté, was staged by the French dancer-choreographer Robert Quinault.

12. Floor plans for productions, 1916–1923, in Boxes 5, 21, 37, 38, 29, 40 (Joseph Urban Papers, Columbia University Library).

13. By December 1912, Carroll and Wayburn had "declared a mutual disagreeing compact," according to an anonymous contributor to *The New York Review* (7 Dec. 1912).

14. The work of Cole Phillips was especially well suited to this treatment, since, at the time he drew only the models' faces and some of the props in detail, while shading the rest of the cover with blocks of color.

15. The climax of this scene was a lighting rather than a choreographic effect. At a musical cue, the conventional stage lights were dimmed and the black lights raised so that the performers' faces disappeared and the stage resembled a lace sampler.

Selected Chronology of Shows Staged by Ned Wayburn

The following is a chronology of 150 of the most important shows staged by Ned Wayburn. The list includes feature acts, musical comedies, revues, and Prologs created between 1899 and 1932.

The following information has been provided for each show when available: place and date of first performance, title of show (with alternative titles, if any), commissioning producer(s), and vaudeville or motion picture theater circuit on which the feature act or Prolog toured. In addition, each show has been identified by type as musical show, revue, pantomime, operetta, act, feature act, or Prolog. Unless otherwise stated, Wayburn received solo credit for each show as "dance director" or "stager."

28 February 1899
By the Sad Sea Waves (musical show)
Dunne and Ryley
Herald Square Theater, New York
NOTE: Wayburn was credited as "stage
    director" and also received credit for
    creating "electrical effects" for the
    dances performed by Agnes Saye.

21 January 1901
The Night of the Fourth (musical show)
Dunne and Ryley
Victoria Theater, New York

25 February 1901
The Governor's Son (musical show)
Hyde and Behrman
Savoy Theater, New York
NOTE: Wayburn was one of five dance
    directors hired and replaced before the
    New York opening of this George M.
    Cohan show. It is likely that the final
    choreography was actually by Cohan,
    although Wayburn occasionally
    included the show on his resumés.

8 June 1901 (week beginning)
The Sunny South (feature act)
Oscar and William Hammerstein
Paradise Garden Roof Theater, New
    York

3 February 1902
The Hall of Fame (musical show)
Sire Brothers
New York Theater, New York

10 February 1902
Miss Simplicity (musical show)
Sire brothers
Casino Theater, New York

26 May 1902 (week beginning)
*The Three CH's (CHic, CHarm and
    CHaste)* (feature act)
Oscar and William Hammerstein
Paradise Garden Roof Theater, New
    York

29 December 1902
The Billionaire (musical show)
Klaw and Erlanger
Daly's Theater, New York

21 January 1903
Mr. Bluebeard (pantomime)
Klaw and Erlanger
Knickerbocker Theater, New Yor
NOTE: Wayburn shared codirection credit
    with Herbert Gresham; Ernest
    d'Auban received credit as "ballet
    master" for the aerial ballets.

27 July 1903
Ned Wayburn's Minstrel Misses
    (feature act)
Klaw and Erlanger
Crystal Garden Theater, New York
Keith Vaudeville Circuit

7 September 1903
The Rogers Brothers in London (musical
    show)
Klaw and Erlanger
Knickerbocker Theater, New York

2 December 1903
Mother Goose (pantomime)
Klaw and Erlanger
New Amsterdam Theater, New York
NOTE: Wayburn shared codirection credit
   with Herbert Gresham.

6 June 1904
A Little Bit of Everything (musical show)
Klaw and Erlanger
New Amsterdam Theater Roof, New
   York

13 June 1904
Ned Wayburn's Girls of 1904
Klaw and Erlanger
New York Theater Roof, New York

20 June 1904 (week beginning)
Ned Wayburn's Rag Sextette
Klaw and Erlanger
New York Theater Roof, New York
Keith Vaudeville Circuit

5 September 1904
The Rogers Brothers in Paris
   (musical show)
Klaw and Erlanger
New Amsterdam Theater, New York

14 November 1904
Humpty-Dumpty (pantomime)
Klaw and Erlanger
New Amsterdam Theater, New York
Note: Wayburn shared codirection credit
   with Herbert Gresham.

21 August 1905
The Pearl and the Pumpkin (pantomime)
Klaw and Erlanger
Broadway Theater, New York

28 August 1905
The Ham Tree (musical show)
Klaw and Erlanger
New York Theater, New York

4 September 1905
The Rogers Brothers in Ireland
   (musical show)
Klaw and Erlanger
New Amsterdam Theater, New York

2 November 1905
The White Cat (pantomime)
Klaw and Erlanger
New Amsterdam Theater, New York

12 May 1906 (week beginning)
The Futurity Winner (feature act)
Headline Vaudeville Production
   Company
Proctor's 58th Street Theater, New York
Keith and Proctor Vaudeville Circuits

31 May 1906
The Rain-dears (feature act)
Headline Vaudeville Production
   Company
Orpheum Theater, Brooklyn
Keith and Proctor Vaudeville Circuits

2 June 1906 (week beginning)
The Daisy Dancers (Dancing Daisies)
   (feature act)
Headline Vaudeville Production
   Company
Proctor's 23rd Street Theater, New York
Keith and Proctor Vaudeville Circuits

6 September 1906 (week beginning)
A One Horse Town (feature act)
Headline Vaudeville Production
   Company
Keith's Theater, Boston
Keith and Proctor Vaudeville Circuits

4 October 1906 (week beginning)
Kitty Town (Kittyland) (feature act)
Headline Vaudeville Production
   Company
Proctor's Novelty Theater, New York
Keith and Proctor Vaudeville Circuits

August–November 1906
The Gainsborough Octette (feature act)
Headline Vaudeville Production
   Company
Proctor's 23rd Street Theater, New York
Keith and Proctor Vaudeville Circuits

August–November 1906
Ned Wayburn's Real Amateurs
   (feature act)
Headline Vaudeville Production
   Company
Proctor's Theater, New York
Keith and Proctor Vaudeville Circuits

5 August 1907
The Phantastic Phantoms (feature act)
Headline Vaudeville Production
   Company
Paradise Garden Roof Theater, New
   York
Keith Vaudeville Circuit

5 August 1907
The Time, the Place and the Girl
   (musical show)
Mortimer H. Singer
Wallack's Theater, New York

2 September 1907
The Rogers Brothers in Panama
   (musical show)
Klaw and Erlanger
Broadway Theater, New York

18 March 1908
The Flower of the Ranch (feature act)
Mortimer H. Singer
West End Theater, New York

23 March 1908
The Honeymoon Trail (musical show)
Mortimer H. Singer
La Salle Theater, Chicago

1 June 1908
Li'l Mose (musical show)
Nixon and Zimmerman
Majestic Theater, Boston

9 July 1908
The Mimic World (musical show)
Lew Fields and the Shubert Brothers
Casino Theater, New York

22 July 1908
Ned Wayburn's Broilers
Headline Vaudeville Production
   Company
Hammerstein's Victoria Theater, New
   York
Keith and Proctor Vaudeville Circuits

3 August 1908
The Girl Question (musical show)
Mortimer H. Singer
Wallack's Theater, New York

5 September 1908
The Girl at the Helm
Mortimer H. Singer
La Salle Theater, Chicago

6 September 1908 (week beginning)
The Star Bout (feature act)
Headline Vaudeville Production
   Company
Proctor's 23rd Street Theater, New York
Keith and Proctor Vaudeville Circuits

28 September 1908
Mlle. Mischief (operetta)
Shubert Brothers
Lyric Theater, New York

14 September 1908
School Days (feature act)
Gus Edwards
Circle Theater, New York

23 December 1908
Mr. Hamlet of Broadway (musical show)
Shubert Brothers
Casino Theater, New York

December 1908
Ned Wayburn's Surf Bathers (feature act)
Headline Vaudeville Production
   Company
Keith and Proctor Vaudeville Circuits

11 February 1909
Havana (musical show)
Shubert Brothers
Casino Theater, New York

16 March 1909
The Golden Girl (musical show)
Mortimer H. Singer
La Salle Theater, Chicago

22 May 1909
The Midnight Sons (musical show)
Lew Fields
Broadway Theater, New York

20 September 1909
The Rose of Algeria
   (musical show/operetta)
Lew Fields
Herald Square Theater, New York

27 September 1909
The Girl and the Wizard (musical show)
Shubert Brothers
Casino Theater, New York

8 November 1909
The Belle of Brittany (operetta)
Shubert Brothers
Daly's Theater, New York

22 November 1909
Old Dutch (musical show)
Lew Fields
Herald Square Theater, New York

22 December 1909
The Goddess of Liberty (musical show)
Mortimer H. Singer
Weber's Music Hall, New York

6 January 1910
The Jolly Bachelors (musical show)
Lew Fields
Broadway Theater, New York

10 January 1910
The King of Caledonia (operetta)
Shubert Brothers
Daly's Theater, New York

13 January 1910
The Prince of Bohemia (operetta)
Shubert Brothers
Hackett Theater, New York

10 February 1910
The Yankee Girl (musical show)
Lew Fields
Herald Square Theater, New York

5 May 1910
Tillie's Nightmare (musical show)
Lew Fields
Herald Square Theater, New York

4 June 1910
The Summer Widowers (musical show)
Lew Fields
Broadway Theater, New York

17 January 1911
The Paradise of Mahomet (musical show)
Lew Fields
Herald Square Theater, New York

4 February 1911
The Hen Pecks (musical show)
Lew Fields
Broadway Theater, New York

12 February 1911
Sweet Sixteen (musical show)
Mortimer H. Singer and William K.
  Ziegfeld
Chicago Opera House

3 April 1911
Love and Politics (musical show)
William K. Ziegfeld
La Salle Theater, Chicago

30 May 1911
The Heart Breakers (musical show)
Mortimer H. Singer
Princess Theater, Chicago

19 August 1911
Hullo Paris (musical show)
Henry Harris and Jesse Laskey
Follies Bergere Theater, New York

22 September 1911
A la Broadway (musical show)
Henry Harris and Jesse Laskey
Follies Bergere Theater, New York

NOTE: After the opening, *A la Broadway*
  was performed as the second act of
  Hullo Paris.

5 October 1911
The Never Homes (musical show)
Lew Fields
Broadway Theater, New York
NOTE: Wayburn shared co-direction
  credit with J.C. Huffman.

2 November 1911
The Wife Hunters (musical show)
Lew Fields
Herald Square Theater, New York

14 February 1912
A Rainy Saturday (feature act)
Mrs. A. Austerlitz [mother of Adele and
  Fred Astaire]
Various vaudeville circuits outside New
  York

19 February 1912 (week beginning)
The Producer (feature act)
Headline Vaudeville Production
  Company
Hammerstein's Victoria Theater, New
  York
Keith Vaudeville Circuit

4 March 1912
Ned Wayburn's English Pony Ballet
  (feature act)
Headline Vaudeville Production
  Company
Alhambra Theater, New York
Orpheum Circuit

22 July 1912
The Passing Show of 1912
  (musical show/revue)
Shubert Brothers
Winter Garden Theater, New York
NOTE: Wayburn did not stage the first
  production on the evening's bill—
  The Ballet of 1830.

11 August 1912
The Military Girl (musical show)
William K. Ziegfeld
Ziegfeld Theater, Chicago

20 November 1912
Broadway to Paris (musical show)
Shubert Brothers
Winter Garden Theater, New York

30 November 1912
The Sun Dodgers (musical show)
Lew Fields
Broadway Theater, New York

6 February 1913
The Honeymoon Express (musical show)
Shubert Brothers
Winter Garden Theater, New York

2 March 1913
The Girls of '61 (feature act)
Headline Vaudeville Production
  Company
Poli's Theater, Westbury, Connecticut
Pantages Vaudeville Circuit

9 May 1913
Eleven Forty-Five (feature act)
Headline Vaudeville Production
  Company
Pantages Vaudeville Circuit
NOTE: The above is the date of copyright.

24 July 1913
The Passing Show of 1913 (musical
  show/revue)
Shubert Brothers
Winter Garden Theater, New York

30 September 1913
Escalade, or The Magic Staircase
  (feature act)
Moss Empires, Ltd.
Hippodrome Theatre, London

28 October 1913
Are You There (musical show/operetta)
Conrad and Zeitlin, Ltd.
Prince of Wales Theatre, London

23 December 1913
Hullo Tango (musical show/revue)
Moss Empires, Ltd.
Hippodrome Theatre, London

13 April 1914
The Honeymoon Express (musical show)
Conrad and Zeitlin, Ltd.
Oxford Theatre, London
NOTE: This show had a different script
  and score from the 1913 New York
  production of the same name.

6 July 1914
Dora's Doze (musical show)
Palladium Music Hall, London

August 1914
The Ham Tree (musical show)
McIntyre and Heath
Theaters in Canada and the American
  West
NOTE: This was a new production of the
  1905 show.

6 December 1914
The Slave Ship (*The Admiral's Daughter*)
  (feature act)
Headline Vaudeville Production
  Company
Hammerstein's Victoria Theater, New
  York
Keith and Orpheum Vaudeville Circuits

25 December 1914
Hello Broaday (musical show)
George M. Cohan
Astor Theater, New York
NOTE: Wayburn staged the following
  numbers only: "Berlin Melodies,"
  "Erie Canal," and "My Flag."

27 February 1915 (week beginning)
The Royal Lilliputian Revue (feature act)
Headline Vaudeville Production
  Company
Wilkes-Barre Opera House, Pennsylva-
  nia
NOTE: This act was commissioned by and
  created for the Singer Midgets.

16 March 1915
She's in Again (musical show)
Headline Vaudeville Production
  Company
Gaiety Theater, New York

5 June 1915
Ziegfeld Midnight Frolics (revue)
Florenz Ziegfeld
New Amsterdam Theater Roof, New
  York

18 June 1915
Splash Me (revue)
Hotel Shelburne Management
Hotel Shelburne, Brighton Beach, New
  York

13 September 1915 (week beginning)
Safety First (feature act)
Headline Vaudeville Production
  Company
Keith's Theater, Philadelphia
Keith Vaudeville Circuit

23 September 1915
Town Topics (musical show/revue)
Headline Vaudeville Production
    Company
Century Theater, New York

24 January 1916
Ziegfeld Midnight Frolics (revue)
Florenz Ziegfeld
New Amsterdam Theater Roof, New
    York

14 May 1916
Melodyland (feature act)
Headline Vaudeville Production
    Company
Paramount-Publix Circuit
Note: The above is the date of copyright.

6 November 1916
The Century Girl (revue)
C.B. Dillingham and Florenz Ziegfeld
Century Theater, New York
NOTE: Wayburn staged only the Act II
    finale, "Uncle Sam's Children."

20 November 1916 (week beginning)
Ned Wayburn's Girlie Gambols
    (feature act)
Headline Vaudeville Production
    Company
Proctor Theater, Yonkers, New York
Orpheum and United Booking Offices

1 December 1916
Ziegfeld Midnight Frolics (revue)
Florenz Ziegfeld
New Amsterdam Theater Roof, New
    York

31 January 1917
Zig Zag (musical show)
Moss Empires, Ltd.
Hippodrome Theatre, London

12 June 1917
Ziegfeld Follies of 1917 (revue)
Florenz Ziegfeld
New Amsterdam Theater, New York

5 November 1917
Miss 1917 (revue)
C. B. Dillingham and Florenz Ziegfeld
Century Theater, New York

29 December 1917
Ziegfeld Midnight Frolics (revue)
Florenz Ziegfeld
New Amsterdam Theater, New York

8 March 1918
Box O'Tricks (musical show)
Moss Empires, Ltd.
Hippodrome Theatre, London

25 April 1918
Follies-Frolic Ball (benefit revue)
Florenz Ziegfeld
New Amsterdam Theater Roof, New
    York

18 June 1918
Ziegfeld Follies of 1918 (revue)
Florenz Ziegfeld
New Amsterdam Theater, New York

19 August 1918
Ziegfeld Midnight Frolics
Florenz Ziegfeld
New Amsterdam Theater Roof, New
    York

10 December 1918
Ziegfeld Midnight Frolic and *Nine
    O'Clock Frolic* (revues)
Florenz Ziegfeld
New Amsterdam Theater Roof, New
    York
NOTE: The two were performed together,
    with the *Nine O'Clock Frolic* serving
    as Act I and the *Midnight Frolic* as Act
    III. Act II was not actually a show, but
    consisted of social dancing by the
    audience and an exhibition ballroom
    team.

25 March 1919
Joy Bells (musical show)
Moss Empires, Ltd.
Hippodrome Theatre, London

16 June 1919
Ziegfeld Follies of 1919 (revue)
Florenz Ziegfeld
New Amsterdam Theater, New York

20 September 1919
The Demi-Tasse Revue (Prolog)
Mesmore Kendall for Metro-Goldwyn-
    Mayer
Capitol Theater, New York
NOTE: Between September 1919 and Jan-
    uary 1920, a new scene was added to
    this Prolog every two weeks, replacing
    an existing scene or specialty act.

18 October 1919
Ziegfeld Midnight Frolics (revue)
Florenz Ziegfeld
New Amsterdam Theater Roof, New
  York

4 January 1920
Ned Wayburn's Song Scenes (Prolog)
Mesmore Kendall for Metro-Goldwyn-
  Mayer
Capitol Theater, New York
NOTE: Between January 1920 and April
  1920, a new scene was added to this
  Prolog every two weeks, replacing an
  existing scene or specialty act.

2 February 1920
The Night Boat (musical show)
C. B. Dillingham
Liberty Theater, New York

8 March 1920
Ziegfeld Midnight Frolics (*The Girls of
  1920*) (revue)
Florenz Ziegfeld
New Amsterdam Theater Roof, New
  York

20 March 1920
Ned Wayburn's Ritz Revue (Prolog)
Mesmore Kendall for Metro-Goldwyn-
  Mayer
Capitol Theater, New York
NOTE: Between April 1920 and the termi-
  nation of Wayburn's contract with the
  Capitol Theater in the summer 1920, a
  new scene was added to this Prolog
  every two weeks, replacing an existing
  scene or specialty act.

5 April 1920
The Ed Wynn Carnival (revue)
A. L. Erlanger and B.C. Whitney
New Amsterdam Theater, New York

3 May 1920
Oui Madame (musical show)
A. L. Erlanger
Majestic Theater, Boston

28 July 1920
The Poor Little Ritz Girl (musical show)
Lew Fields
Central Theater, New York

19 October 1920
Hitchy-Koo of 1920 (revue)
C. B. Dillingham for Raymond
  Hitchcock
New Amsterdam Theater, New York

17 November 1920
Jimmie (musical show)
Morosco Holding Company
Apollo Theater, New York

29 November 1920
Vogues and Vanities of 1920 (revue)
Majestic Theater, Boston

4 September 1921
Town Gossip (musical show)
Headline Vaudeville Production
  Company
Ford's Opera House, Baltimore,
  Maryland

3 May 1921
Two Little Girls in Blue (musical show)
A. L. Erlanger
George M. Cohan Theater, New York

22 January 1922
Little Kangaroo (musical show)
Morosco Holding Company
Stamford Theater, Stamford, Connecti-
  cut

5 June 1922
Ziegfeld Follies of 1922 (musical show)
Florenz Ziegfeld
New Amsterdam Theater, New York

15 October 1922
Ned Wayburn's Dancing Dozens
  (Prolog)
Headline Vaudeville Production
  Company
Famous Player-Laskey Circuit

18 January 1923 (week beginning)
The Capitol Demi-Tasse (Prolog)
Headline Vaudeville Production
  Company
Famous Player-Laskey Circuit
NOTE: This Prolog, which had different
  acts from its namesake, seemed to be
  cashing in on the Capitol Theater
  name.

22 January 1923
Lady Butterfly (musical show)
Morosco Holding Company
Globe Theater, New York

5 March 1923
Simonette (The Birth of Venus)
 (Prolog tableau)
Ned Wayburn and Ben Ali Haggin
Palace Theater, New York
Paramount-Publix Circuit

5 March 1923
Anatole Friedland Revue of 1923
 (Prolog)
Anatole Friedland
Famous Players-Laskey Circuit

5 March 1923
Makin' Believe (Prolog)
Headline Vaudeville Production
 Company
Keith's Fordham Theater, Bronx, New
 York
Keith-Albee-Orpheum Theater Circuit

20 May 1923
*Ned Wayburn's Demi-Tasse Revue
 of 1923* (revue)
Hotel Shelburne Management
Hotel Shelburne, Brighton Beach, New
 York

28 June 1923
Ned Wayburn's Song Scenes of 1923
 (revue)
Hotel Shelburne Management
Hotel Shelburne, Brighton Beach, New
 York

25 August 1923
Ned Wayburn's Moonlite Show (revue)
Hotel Shelburne Management
Hotel Shelburne, Brighton Beach, New
 York

20 October 1923
Ziegfeld Follies of 1923
Florenz Ziegfeld
New Amsterdam Theater, New York

18 February 1923
Ned Wayburn's Honeymoon Cruise
 (Prolog)
Headline Vaudeville Production
 Company
Palace Theater, New York
Paramount-Publix Circuit

February 1924
Ned Wayburn's Symphonic Jazz Revue
 (Prolog)
Headline Vaudeville Production
 Company
Paramount-Publix Circuit

March 1925
Carmen: An Operatic Fantasie
 (feature act)
Geraldine Ferrar
Paramount-Publix Circuit

23 May 1925
Fez (Prolog Tableau)
Ned Wayburn and Ned Ali Haggin
Paramount-Publix Circuit
NOTE: The above is the date of copyright.

25 November 1925
The Maiden Voyage (Prolog)
Headline Vaudeville Production
 Company
Stamford Theater, Stamford, Connecti-
 cut
Paramount-Publix Circuit

14 January 1926
Palm Beach Night (musical show)
Florenz Ziegfeld
Montmartre Club, Palm Beach, Florida

June 1926
Cupid's Holiday (Prolog tableau)
Ned Wayburn and Ben Ali Haggin
Paramount-Publix Circuit

13 September 1926
Ned Wayburn's Variety Show (Prolog)
Headline Vaudeville Production
 Company
Poli's Palace Theater, Bridgeport,
 Connecticut
Paramount-Publix Circuit

April 1927
Ned Wayburn's Buds of 1927 (Prolog)
Headline Vaudeville Production
 Company
Paramount-Publix Circuit

18 September 1927
Ned Wayburn's Ritzy Revue (Prolog)
Headline Vaudeville Production
 Company
Poli's Palace Theater, Bridgeport,
 Connecticut
Paramount-Publix Circuit

April 1928
Ned Wayburn's Buds of 1928 (Prolog)
Headline Vaudeville Production
 Company
Poli's Palace Theater, Bridgeport,
 Connecticut
Paramount-Publix Circuit

19 May 1928
Ned Wayburn's Chicks (Prolog)
Headline Vaudeville Production
    Company
New Stanley Theater, Jersey City, New
    Jersey
Paramount-Publix Circuit

26 November 1928
Ned Wayburn's Gambols (Prolog)
Headline Vaudeville Production
    Company
Court Square Theater, Springfield,
    Massachusetts
Paramount-Publix Circuit

18 November 1930
Smiles (musical show)
Florenz Ziegfeld
Ziegfeld Theater, New York
NOTE: Ned Wayburn is believed to have
    "doctored" this show, especially the
    chorus routines.

30 March 1931
Town Talk (Prolog)
Ned Wayburn
Poli's Palace Theater, Bridgeport,
    Connecticut
Paramount-Publix Circuit

31 March 1932
Ned Wayburn's Gigolettes (feature act)
Ned Wayburn
RKO Proctor's Theater, Yonkers, New
    York
Keith-Albee-Orpheum Theater Circuit

28 October 1932
Ned Wayburn's Girl Revue (Prolog)
Ned Wayburn
Capitol Theater, Bayside, Queens, New
    York

November 1932
*Ned Wayburn's Modern Rhythm
    Dancers* (act)
Ned Wayburn
Rex Théâtre, Paris

Ned Wayburn's Notated Dance Instructions

The introductory lessons and individual dance routines created and approved by Ned Wayburn are among the most important surviving examples of his dance idioms, teaching methods, and choreography. Like so many of his colleagues in the period, Wayburn notated lessons and dances for sale both to amateur dancers and to teachers.

"Ned Wayburn's Home-Study Course in Stage Dancing" was published by the Wayburn Studios of Stage Dancing in 1926. It was available on a mail order subscription basis and was widely advertised in periodicals as a health and beauty aid, as well as a route to a possible dance career. The two sets of lessons reprinted her show the intense rate of learning and the practice necessary to follow the plan. Lessons 1-5 of the Foundation Technique include stage orientation, tap basics, and foot articulation. Lessons 41-45 introduce Ballet Technique, moving from the basic foot and arm positions to pliés.

Wayburn himself taught at the Dance Masters of America Annual Normal Course and Convention in August 1926. The Acrobatic High Kicking Routine included here, which could be performed by a single dancer, couple, or precision line, was one of many routines distributed in mimeographed form to the attending teachers. The notated dances from the 1926 to 1941 Annual Courses were donated to the Dance Collection by Catherine B. Sullivan.

The "Savannah Stomp" is an example of Wayburn choreography notated and published in contemporary periodicals, in this case the March 1928 issue of *The Dance Magazine*. The Stomp was an eccentric tap and step solo performed in the open lunge associated with musical comedy stars such as Ann Pennington and Frances White.

Wayburn's exhibition ballroom choreography was taught and sold extensively in the 1920s in many formats. Like Ruth St. Denis, Ted Shawn, Alexis Kosloff, and others, Wayburn licensed Ampico, the American Piano Company, to sell dance instructions with rolls for its reproducing pianos. The "Ballroom Charleston" reproduced below is from a Wayburn series for which no rolls have been located. It is followed by his "Original 'Footloose' Strut." Set to a fox trot with a cha-cha rhythm, the dance was published on the back cover of the sheet music for "Footloose," a song by Hal Cochran and Carl Rupp that promoted the film serial of the same name.

Ned Wayburn's Home-Study Course in Stage Dancing. Copyright 1925 by Ned Wayburn Studios of Stage Dancing. Reproduced from a copy in the collection of A. J. Pischl.

LESSONS 1 TO 5
Foundation Technique

YOUR ROOM IS YOUR STAGE

You are going to learn stage dancing. And you are going to learn it right in your room at home! Your room is your stage!

A large dancing floor is not needed to learn stage dancing. It differs in this respect from most social dancing. Social, or ball-room dancing is usually a "traveling" step, and works out the nicest when you can go around and around a big ball room.

But stage dancing is done in a smaller space and traveling steps are used chiefly to get the dancer on and off the stage. For this reason you can learn stage dancing at home in your own room, quite as well as you could in a large dance hall.

Any smooth floor will serve for your practice. It should <u>not</u> be covered with a rug or a carpet. The only furniture needed will be a straight light chair to lean on in your first practice. A full length mirror, while not essential, is highly desirable.

This room in which you are to work represents your stage on which you are dancing. One wall of your room represents the curtain line of the stage, beyond which is the audience. You are to learn to dance for that audience, and if you have a large mirror and can have it hung in the center of one side of your room, then, as you dance, you can see yourself in the mirror as you appear to the audience.

In this course there will be very little matter for you to sit down and read or study. The instructions are practical and apply immediately to actual dancing and to exercises to develop your muscles for dancing. Therefore you will want your lessons available right in your practice room. You will want them immediately before your eyes as you learn and practice the exercises and dancing steps.

To make these lessons the most convenient for you to use and to keep, I have had them arranged in these long sheets, and printed on one side of the paper only. This is done so you can take these sheets and either hold them folded in your hand, or stretch them out and fasten them on your wall with thumb tacks. Thus you will be able to see the instructions and drawings right before your eyes as you do your work—a plan that I am sure will help you.

But do not let the fact that I have assembled these lessons in large sheets in this fashion cause you to try to rush through a whole series at once. Take up the lessons one at a time and carefully master each one, item by item, before taking up the next lesson. Be <u>thorough</u> and get it in your head as you go, and also into your feet. I mean, practice the movements, exercises or steps until you perfect them, before going on with the next lesson.

With the instructions, drawings and phonograph records which I am sending, you will have no excuse for not getting everything <u>thoroughly</u> as you go along. No one is rushing you, and you can take your time. If you learn quickly you will have more time for review and practice work. But if you are a little slower at learning, you still have a chance to study each lesson or each step until you master it.

In this respect, you, as a home study pupil, really have an advantage over those taking such work in schools, where one pays for the instructor's time. There, if the work given is in individual private lessons, the instructor's time is expensive. If it is in class work, it is less expensive, but the class cannot be delayed for you in case you find some step unusually difficult, and fail to get it right away. In home study work, it will be your own fault, if you fail to master all of the work thoroughly as you go.

LESSON ONE

POSITION

Stand in the center of your room in POSITION. Position means that the body should be erect, the head up, eyes looking straight to the front, the hands hanging at your sides, body relaxed so that there is no tension on your muscles. You should be facing the side of the room which you have decided is to be the front of your stage.

YOUR PLACE

Your heels should be together, and your toes should be pointed out at an angle of 45 degrees. The place where you stand on the floor is YOUR PLACE. Picture it as a circle drawn around your feet. In dancing it is necessary to have an accurate sense of direction on the stage. So picture "YOUR PLACE" in the center of your room, and always start your exercises or dances from POSITION in YOUR PLACE, unless you are definitely instructed to do otherwise.

POSITION

YOUR PLACE

THE EIGHT STAGE DIRECTIONS

Now stand in position in your place and face the side of your room which represents the front of your stage. The direction you are facing is FRONT, and that wall is the front of your stage. The direction to your left is LEFT, and toward that wall is STAGE LEFT. The direction behind you is BACK, and that wall is the back of your stage. The direction to your right is RIGHT, and toward that wall is STAGE RIGHT.

From your position, facing front, turn to your left until you face the front left corner of the room. The direction you are now facing is LEFT OBLIQUE.

In making a turn around to your left, you should carry the weight of the body on the right heel, the left foot being slightly raised from the floor. As you turn, the right heel acts as a pivot holding you in your place (the same spot). In turning around to the right, pivot on the left heel. From your LEFT OBLIQUE position turn again to the left till you face LEFT. Now turn again till you face the left rear corner. You are now facing LEFT OBLIQUE BACK.

```
        8
     FRONT
 1  LEFT      RIGHT  7
    OBLIQUE   OBLIQUE

LEFT  <--------->  RIGHT
 2                   6

   LEFT         RIGHT
 3 OBLIQUE      OBLIQUE 5
   BACK         BACK
       BACK
        4
```
8 STAGE DIRECTIONS

Turn further to your left around until you face BACK. Turn again until you face the right rear corner of the room, this direction is RIGHT OBLIQUE BACK. Turn further and face the RIGHT. Turn further and face the right front corner which is RIGHT OBLIQUE. Finish the complete turn and again face FRONT.

These eight stage directions are important. You must know them. You must be able to go into any room, and choosing one side to represent the FRONT, be able instantly to turn to any of these stage directions, or to step, kick, turn your head, or point your hand to any one of these directions without hesitating or making errors. Now make the same series of turns again to your left, and call off each stage direction as you face it. Then make a similar series of turns to your right, pivoting on your left heel. After you have practiced these simpler turns, try calling off the stage directions at random, as "LEFT," "RIGHT OBLIQUE," "BACK," "LEFT OBLIQUE BACK," "FRONT," "RIGHT OBLIQUE BACK," etc., and each time turn immediately the direction called. Master the directions thoroughly before taking up the next lesson.

LESSON TWO

THE FOUR PARTS OF THE FOOT

For the purpose of instruction in dancing, I divide the foot into four parts:
TOE, BALL, HEEL, FLAT.

The TOE is the end of the shoe.

The BALL is the half sole — the part of the foot on which the weight rests when
you raise the heel from the floor.

The HEEL is the heel of your foot, and of your shoe.

The FLAT is both the sole and the heel, on which the weight rests
together as you ordinarily stand.

These terms for the four parts of the foot are also used to indicate
the way the foot strikes the floor.

TOE

Stand in position in your place. Raise the left foot up behind you
and then drop it down and strike the floor with the toe of your left
shoe. The most natural direction in which to do this is back, or
behind the position that the foot occupied in place. This makes a
sound which I call a "TOE-TAP."

Now strike the floor with the ball of the left foot, in place. This
sound I call a "STRAIGHT-TAP."

BALL

Strike the floor with the heel of the left foot, in place. This
sound I call a "HEEL-TAP."

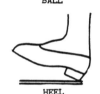

Strike the floor with the flat of the left foot, that is step
straight down so that the ball and the heel strike the floor at
the same time, in place. Put your weight on the left foot. This
sound I call a "FLAT-TAP."

HEEL

Lift the <u>right</u> foot from the floor and tap with the
toe, ball, heel, flat.

Then do eight taps to a regular time, or rhythm, counting: (LEFT) toe,
ball, heel, flat; (RIGHT) toe, ball, heel, flat. Repeat and count
these taps, counting from one to eight; always begin with the left

FLAT   toe-tap.

Practice these simple taps always counting to eight and repeating. Beat a regular
smooth musical rhythm with the sound of these taps on the floor.

Also continue to practice your eight stage directions: Thus, stand in position facing
FRONT: without turning your body, turn your face to the RIGHT. Face FRONT again,
turn your body to LEFT OBLIQUE and turn your face to the LEFT. Note carefully that
the stage directions are the directions on the stage, or of your room, as determined
by your right and left when you were facing FRONT. When you are facing BACK your
right hand is toward stage LEFT. When you are facing FRONT you would turn to your
left to face stage LEFT; but if you were facing BACK and told to face stage LEFT you
would do so by turning to your right. You must get the stage direction so thoroughly
in mind that you will know them instinctively no matter in what position you may be,
or how you may turn.

LESSON THREE

THE TAPS

STRAIGHT TAP

I have given you the four parts of the foot and shown you how each part of the foot can be used to tap or strike the floor. These taps are all used in dancing, but the more frequently used taps are those made with the ball of the foot, and they can be made in three different ways.

The ball of the foot can strike the floor by bringing it straight down. This is known as the STRAIGHT TAP. Stand in position, heels together; raise left foot about two inches and tap straight down in place. Do eight of these straight taps with the left foot, then shift weight, raising right foot, do eight straight taps with the right.

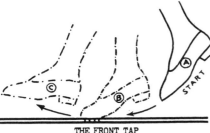
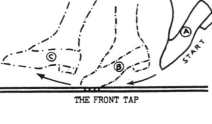

THE FRONT TAP

The ball of the foot can also be made to strike the floor as the foot is swinging forward and this is known as the FRONT TAP. Stand in position with your heels together. Raise the left foot about two inches from the floor bending the knee slightly; swing the foot back a little. Now swing the lower leg (from knee down) forward and as it swings let the ball of the foot strike the floor with a sharp tap. It is the inside edge of the sole that strikes the harder. The ankle is held loose and as the foot strikes the floor it rebounds a little, making a sharp clear tapping sound. The foot should not scrape, drag or shuffle. After making the front tap the foot is in the air. You cannot make a front tap and have the foot remain on the floor--that would be a straight tap.

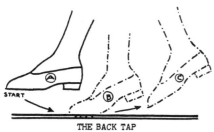

THE BACK TAP

Beginning with the left foot, practice this front tap, striking the floor as the foot swings forward and clearing the floor as the foot swings back. Count the taps from one to seven, make count "eight" a flat tap in which the foot remains on the floor and takes the weight, and on the count "one" that follows, make the front tap with the right foot, and continue, alternating the feet after each eight counts.

The BACK TAP is made by striking the ball of the foot as the foot is moving backwards. Practice this exactly as you did the front tap except that as you swing the foot forward, it clears the floor; tap it as it swings backward. Count the same, beginning with the left, making the eighth count a straight tap and changing to right, etc.

THE HEEL TAP

These two taps, in various combinations, form a large part of Tap and Step dancing. You must perfect them so they are sharp clear taps, and not shuffling sounds—and that requires practice!

The HEEL TAP is simpler and is less used. Practice it as follows: Stand in position, raise left foot and count as you tap seven times with the left heel, on "eight" come down with a flat tap, shifting weight to the left and make seven heel taps with the right and finish on the flat of right foot on the eighth count. This is good practice for acquiring balance.

LESSON FOUR

THE HOPS

Before giving you the tap combinations, I want you to practice the hops. Stand in position with the heels raised from the floor. Raise the right foot up behind, off the floor, then hop from the floor with the left foot and light on the left foot-- that is a hop, when you jump from the floor with one foot and light on the same foot. In alighting come down on the ball of the foot only, with the knee slightly bent; never land the weight on the heel or with the knee stiff, for the jarring would be very injurious. It shocks your nervous system to land stiff-legged.

Put dance record No. 1 on your phonograph and try hopping around your room to music. Hop on the left, step on the right, hop on right, step on left, hop on left, etc. Then change to this: hop twice on left, step on right, hop twice on right, step on left, hop twice on left, etc. Also try hopping four times, and later eight times on each foot before changing. This simple hopping around the room to music is a very good test of dancing ability, and I frequently use this test with a large number of people from whom I must pick out quickly the more capable dancers, by observing the way they keep time and control their balance.

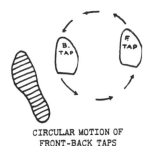

CIRCULAR MOTION OF
FRONT-BACK TAPS

COMBINING THE TAPS

The FRONT and the BACK taps when combined in one action is the FRONT-BACK TAP, and is also called a ROLL. In making this combination tap, the foot should swing in a circle as shown in the drawing. Make a front tap as foot swings forward, then circling it out and back and make the back tap as it swings backward. The time is the same as making the front or back tap separately, but now you tap as the foot swings both ways so there are two tap sounds to each count or beat of the music. We count this with an "and" count: "And" on the front tap, "one" on the back tap, "and" on the front tap, "two" on the back tap, etc.

Now practice this, beginning with the left foot, counting "and" for the front taps and the numbered counts on the back taps. On the count of "eight" make a flat tap, that is the foot strikes the floor as it comes back and remains on the floor, taking the weight. Follow with the same series on the right foot, again making a flat tap on the count of eight and changing to left, etc.

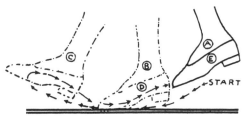

ACTION OF FOOT IN FRONT-BACK TAPS

The FRONT-BACK-STRAIGHT tap combines these three actions on a single beat of the music and is counted "and-a-one," "and-a- two," etc. Tap front on the sound of "and," tap back on the sound of "a" and tap straight on the "one." Strong accent on the count of one.

Practice this two ways, first do eight of these combinations with the left, eight of them with the right. Later, after you have acquired a little more speed, alter- nate the feet at each count; "and-a-one" with the left, "and-a-two" with the right, "and-a-three" with the left, etc.

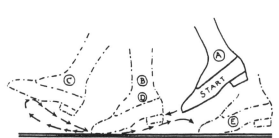

ACTION OF FOOT IN FRONT-BACK-STRAIGHT TAPS

LESSON FIVE

COMBINING TAPS AND HOPS

BACK, STRAIGHT, HOP

You should now have your taps perfected so you can combine them with hops. There
are two exceedingly important combinations for you to know--and to know well.
Every dancer will, at some time or other, have to do these in routines. Practice
carefully and diligently until you have perfected them. The first one is the
BACK, STRAIGHT, HOP, which is done as follows: Stand in position; back tap with
the left foot, straight tap with left foot, hop on the left foot, at same time
right foot travels to RIGHT OBLIQUE. Reverse. Back tap with the right foot,
straight tap with the right foot, hop on the right foot, at same time the left
foot travels to LEFT OBLIQUE. The count is "a-one-hop, a-two-hop, a-three-hop".

FRONT-BACK, HOP, STRAIGHT

The second combination is a FRONT-BACK tap, HOP, and a STRAIGHT tap. Make the
front-back tap with the left foot, and while the foot is in the air behind, hop with
the right foot, then bring the left foot down with a straight tap. Now follow with a
right front-back, left hop, right straight. This combination gives four tapping sounds
and this is too many to be counted a single numbered count, so you count it like this:
Count "and-a-one" for the left front-back and the right hop, count "two" for the left
straight, count "and-a-three" for the right front-back and the left hop, and count
"four" for the right straight.

THE "TIME STEP" AND THE "BREAK"

The Time Step and the Break may be considered the keys to buck dancing. These movements are considerably more advanced than the exercises I have been giving you, and
you will need to work hard to get them. But I want you to learn them now and practice
them constantly to prepare for the Tap and Step dancing. Note that the Time Step and
the Break start the same but end differently. Learn each one separately and then put
the two together. Note that the Time Step goes to eight counts but the Break only
to seven counts. That is why we call it a break, you stop dancing one count short of
the musical phrase and so get a break in your dance, much like a "rest" in music.
The counts of these dances give you the rhythm as near as it can be given by counting,
but after you have learned the action of the dance you will perfect the rhythm from
the phonograph record which gives the exact sounds made by your feet in perfect time.

THE TIME STEP		THE BREAK	
Count	The action	Count	The action
And	Front tap with right foot	And	Front tap with right foot
A	Back tap with right	A	Back tap with right
ONE	Hop on left, accent strongly	ONE	Hop on left, accent strongly
TWO	Straight on right, takes weight	TWO	Straight on right, takes weight
And	Front tap with left	And	Front tap with left
THREE	Straight tap with left	THREE	Back tap with left
FOUR	Straight tap on right, accent strongly		
		And	Straight tap with left
And	Front tap with left	FOUR	Straight on right, takes weight
A	Back tap with left		
ONE	Hop on right, accent strongly	FIVE	Hop on right, accent strongly
		And	Front tap with left
TWO	Straight on left, takes weight	SIX	Straight with left a little to front
And	Front tap with right		
THREE	Straight tap with right	And	Straight tap with right
FOUR	Straight on left, accent strongly	SEVEN	Flat tap with left, accent strongly

CONSTANT PRACTICE NECESSARY TO SUCCESS IN DANCING

What I have taught you in these first five lessons is very necessary to your
success as a dancer. It is very simple, just the few matters of the directions
on the stage and a few taps to be made with different parts of the foot. You could
learn it all in an hour or two, if you merely needed to learn it so you could
show others what was meant by "left oblique back" or a "front-back-straight" tap.

But you will never become a dancer just by learning what these things mean. Instead
you must learn them till they become second nature to you or instinctive in your
mind, so your feet respond immediately.

If you are being taught a dance routine and a stage direction is given you must be
able to turn to that direction without stopping to think about it or hardly realizing
what you are doing. That is why I give these directions to you at the very beginning
of your course, so that you can at once learn them perfectly, and then they will not
confuse you in your later work.

I then followed with the "parts of the foot" and the various taps and simple combinations of them. These are the very elements of dancing just as A B C are the
elements of spelling and reading. You must know these taps so that doing them becomes
automatic to your feet. Later, when you come to take up tap and step dancing you won't
have time to think out how to make a front tap, or a front-back, or a front-hop-straight.
But you must be able to make these taps without stopping to think, automatically, so
that you can give your attention to the more advanced elements of the routines.

The only way to learn these taps so that you can do them in this easy fashion, is by
constant practice. You must therefore keep on practicing these tap combinations each
day during the coming weeks while you are taking up and learning the heavier movements
of my Limbering and Stretching work, which will develop your body for the more
complicated dancing steps you will have later on.

Do not let interest in the new work that is coming cause you to neglect keeping up
faithful daily practice of this important tapping work. The Time Step and Break as
given you in Lesson Five are not easy, and constant practice on these each day, during
the period that you are taking the Limbering and Stretching work, will be needed to
prepare you for going ahead with Tap and Step dancing (which you will take up in
Lesson Twenty-one).

I will leave you to judge the amount of time you can devote to practice each day, as
of course that will depend on how busy you are with other matters. But you can't
become an expert dancer unless you are really sufficiently interested to keep up
faithful practice every day and devote all the time to it that you can spare from
other work or duties. Of the time you have available, I would suggest that you can
well afford to spend at least one fourth of it, during the next six weeks, to this
mastering of tapping, and that three-fourths of your time should be devoted to the
Limbering and Stretching work.

It may not be quite as interesting for you now to spend hours and hours just learning to
do a few combinations of taps and hops as it would be to go to some social dance, but
you have this thought to console you: Later on when your friends are still doing their
same old social dances in the same old way you will be doing dances of a professional
calibre that will be the envy of all of them. Expert dancing which brings you fame and
money cannot be learned just by dancing for the fun of it. Success in any line of
endeavor comes only from work, and not from playing around and dabbling with it. But
real work brings success and that will be much more fun in the long run!

LESSONS 41 TO 45
Ballet Technique
Foot and Arm Positions—Bar Work

BALLET

My Americanized Ballet is divided into specialized types such as "Toe" "Classical" "Character" and "Interpretative Dancing" and in the next set of twenty lessons, I'm going to give you Modern Technique which will prepare you for any one of these special types of work. The Ballet as taught in my school differs from European Ballet in that the work is condensed and concentrated so that one need not spend years and years studying before giving public performances.

Since the ancient days—hundreds of years ago—when the primitive peoples danced whenever their emotions were deeply moved, the days when every ceremony of importance was conducted with dancing from the rites of religion, weddings, funerals, feasts to the rites of public triumphs, victories in war and in the theatre; since the days when the seed of dancing that was planted in Egypt and flowered in Greece reached full bloom in France under the reign of Louis XIV in the Ballet; since those days there has come a time when the world turned away from all arts and Dancing, lost its hold on the people and was apparently forgotten. But because dancing is one of the most natural and most elementary of the arts, there were a few Dance lovers who simultaneously unknown to one another, began to recreate the dance to suit the modern times. Some years ago these few great dancers returned to give back to the world—The Dance.

Great exponents of the dance brought back a new art to the stage. By subtle gesture, by beautiful technique, they developed a symbolic art that evoked the exquisite memories of childhood and aroused beauties within, allowing us to seek the free expression of delicate feelings—feelings that we had hardly knew existed in our unemotional lives! Then came the first creators of the dramatic pantomime in modern form in the Dance—frankly dramatic, who, with their vivid personality, grace and beauty of motion influenced the modern dance, bringing us in touch with the mysterious East, stirring our imaginations until we wanted to discover the ways and thoughts of a land so different from our own.

Close on the heels of dramatic pantomime came the Russian Ballet. Through the work of Russian Ballet there was restored to our dull drab life, color and thrills. It searched far into our emotional souls and urged us to lay aside our false pride and respond to nature's truths with simplicity and beauty.

And then—then we saw Anna Pavlowa—Pavlowa the incomparable! who has given to the dance not only delicacy and beauty but dramatic intensity filled with ecstatic wild joy! She not only purified Symbolic Art but glorified the Art of Freedom and Power.
"It is thru the dance that rhythm will return to life. Who has not felt the longing to dance, to run, to leap, to toss the arms for joy—to express our melancholy in slow and swaying rhythms."

With such influence is it any wonder that I so desire to carry on their work by constantly reviving and recreating the dance to fit the modern trends; by studying the needs of the world for this art, and devoting my whole life to the Art of the Dance?

It is Americanized Ballet Technique in which we are most interested now. To accomplish the desired ends in this work requires Infinite Patience—Untiring Practice on your part. Do not slight the beginning lessons! Every exercise is of infinite value and I can't emphasize enough the necessity of learning perfectly each exercise as you come to it. Do not skip one day's work because the next looks more exciting. The exercises are arranged so that every new exercise depends upon the preceding ones!

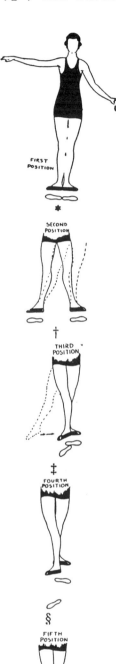

FIRST
POSITION

SECOND
POSITION

†

THIRD
POSITION

‡

FOURTH
POSITION

§

FIFTH
POSITION

¶

LESSON FORTY-ONE

FIVE POSITIONS OF THE FEET

The Five Positions of the feet and the Five Positions of the
arms are the fundamentals of all Ballet dancing. As they
are the basis for all the following work, it is advisable
to be letter perfect in each position, to have an accurate
position knowledge of each one before attempting any Bar work.

* FIRST POSITION: Stand erect, head up, legs straight, heels
together, toes pointed out making a straight line with the
feet ; the weight of the body evenly distributed between the
two feet. Lightly grasp the bar with one hand, carrying the
other arm out straight from the shoulder, slightly relaxed
as shown in diagram. Holding the bar will control your balance.

† SECOND POSITION: From the first position, keep both legs
straight and slide right foot sideways until the leg and foot
are fully extended without moving the body. Then place the
weight of body on both feet. Keep the heels on the floor.
The head should be in a straight line above the center of space
between the heels.

‡ THIRD POSITION: From the second position, shift the weight
to one leg, fully extending the foot and toes of the other leg.
Then glide the extended leg slowly in front of the supporting
leg, the heel leading until heel is in centre of supporting
foot.

§ FOURTH POSITION: From the third position, slide the front
leg forward as far as possible without moving the body, until
foot and toes are fully extended ; then, put heel on floor,
foot out in a straight line. Place weight of body on both
legs. The head should be vertically above the heel of the front
foot. Keep both knees straight.

¶ FIFTH POSITION: From the fourth position shift weight to
the back leg full extending the front leg and foot. Slide the
front leg slowly back to other leg, heel turned well out,
until heel is in front of toes of the back leg. The weight
of the body should rest on both legs, both knees should be
straight. The throat should be vertically above the ankle
of the front leg.

Note: You will find these positions difficult to hold but by
constant practice you will soon be more at ease. Try
to get each position as perfect as possible without
straining yourself. Remember the knees must be kept
straight—the back must be kept straight, the
head must be kept high.

LESSON FORTY-TWO

FIVE POSITIONS OF THE ARMS

There are five fundamental arm positions. As I've told you, it is most vital to dance with the whole body and not just the feet, therefore you must learn the few governing rules for the arms and hands and body, applying them throughout your training. In all arms positions, keep the hands and arms softly relaxed, the line from the shoulder to the finger tips forming a continuous flowing line. This line may curve but must never be a sharp bend, nor a sag. The wrists and elbows often get themselves into ugly angles, which not only ruin the flowing lines of the arms but spoil the effect of the dance.

Unless otherwise designated, the palms of the hand should always be turned in toward the body. When moving the arm from one position to another be sure to turn the hand only the moment before the arm reaches the desired position. The wrists should always lead the movement, the hand following.

* FIRST POSITION: Hold arms out in front of you. Curve them loosely in flowing continuous lines—elbows not sagging nor bent, lines not broken at the wrists—as if you were holding a big bouquet of flowers. The tip of the second finger should curve near the end of the thumb, the first and ring fingers should be slightly bent and the little finger extended from the others.

† SECOND POSITION: From the first position, bring arms to sides, extending them in a straight line from the shoulders, palms down.

‡ THIRD POSITION: (A). From the second position, raise one arm above the head, elbows slightly curved to make a soft graceful line, palm turned in. Extend the other arm to the side as in second position. This is Third Position A because it is a closed position. By a closed position, I mean that the palms are turned in.

§ THIRD POSITION: (B). The Third Position B is exactly the same as (A) except that the raised arm should be turned outward, palm out and the other arm extended to the side, palm down. This is called an open position.

¶ FOURTH POSITION: This position is a combination of the third position and the first position—that is, one arm is raised palm in and the other is held loosely in front of you palm in toward body.

* FIFTH POSITION: (A). In the Fifth Position both arms are raised above the head. Palms are turned in, arms are slightly curved but not bent. The arms should be raised so that it is possible by raising the eyes to look into the palms of the hands which are turned down. The line should not be broken from the shoulder to the finger tips. This is a <u>closed</u> position.

† FIFTH POSITION: (B). Fifth Position B is exactly like A except that it is an <u>open</u> position, that is, arms raised with the wrists curved and the line broken, palms turned outward, forming a figure similar to the letter <u>V.</u>

LESSON FORTY-THREE

Before we take up the Bar Exercises, in which you will use combinations of the foot and arm positions, I want you to combine the FIRST FOOT POSITION with the FIRST ARM POSITION, SECOND FOOT POSITION with the SECOND ARM POSITION, etc. If you practice these rigorously you will develop beauty of line and motion and you will be able to slide into a position when it is named without any thought. <u>Each time you take a position content yourself only with the best lines that you can create—the most charming and graceful that you can obtain.</u> Improving each day will be the best way to acquire perfect poise and grace in Ballet work.

COMBINATION OF FOOT AND ARM POSITIONS

Stand in FIRST FOOT POSITION—heels together, toes pointed out, making straight line with the feet. Curve the arms in front of you in FIRST ARM POSITION.

Change into SECOND FOOT POSITION. Slide right foot to the side until fully extended, toe pointed—then heel to the floor, weight evenly distributed. Extend arms into SECOND ARM POSITION.

Slide into THIRD FOOT POSITION, raising arm (opposite arm to the foot that is in FRONT should be the raised arm) into THIRD ARM POSITION A a closed position.

Hold the THIRD FOOT POSITION. Change from THIRD ARM POSITION A TO THIRD ARM POSITION B, which is an open position.

CHANGE INTO FOURTH FOOT POSITION by sliding the front leg forward until fully extended—place the weight on both legs, arms moving into FOURTH ARM POSITION, one arm loosely raised, the other held in front as in first position.

From Fourth Position change into FIFTH FOOT POSITION and form frame for the face with arms in FIFTH ARM POSITION A. Keep feet in FIFTH FOOT POSITON while the arms take the FIFTH ARM POSITION B in an open position, or palms turned outwards.

Note: Repeat these combinations until you are familiar with them.

BAR EXERCISES

Bar exercises must be done everyday for fifteen or twenty minutes preceding the floor exercises. The Bar exercises teach the muscles to coordinate, teach the legs to mind the will, teach the arms to obey, and whole body to respond to your desires as a dancer.

Don't expect to do each one of these exercises perfectly at first. When you take into the consideration the fact that for many years your arms and legs have performed only a few variations of motion and that there are many unused muscles which need to be developed, you will be extremely patient and realize that it is going to take time and a good deal of honest practice to teach these muscles how to behave and how to mind the will that controls them.

Persist in your efforts even if you feel sore and stiff. All the first soreness will work out "if you don't let it get you". It is constant steady work that will ease up the muscles and relieve lameness. Above all, at the beginning "DON'T OVERDO it," but rather increase the work as your strength and limberness permit.

Keep in mind the following when doing your bar exercises.

When you KICK push the leg as high as it will go. Do not strain or force it up but stretch it as far as you possibly can. Keep the knees straight, toes pointed, and back straight.

When you POINT YOUR TOE, point it DOWN and OUT. Feel the muscles stretching. This will strengthen your ankles. Your toes should always point when off the floor.

Do not exercise carelessly. Careless work is worse than useless. Put all the energy you can into all of your exercises.

LESSON FORTY-FOUR

The first exercise that I am to teach you is called "Grand Plie and Relever", being a combination of "plies" (knee-bends) and "relevers" (risings on balls of feet).

RELEVER
(Ray-l ay-vey)

The first exercise given you in the Limbering and Stretching Exercise was actually a "relever" although we did not name it such. This French term means to rise; the Ballet term means to rise on the ball of the foot as far as possible. bending the arch well out. and keeping the knees straight.

This exercise develops the ankles and calves of the leg, removing all surplus fat from them, and strengthens the arch of the foot. Stand in FIRST POSITION, left hand holding bar.

PREPARATION EXERCISE

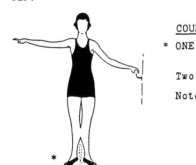

COUNTS

* ONE   Rise on balls of the feet, turning the arch well out, keeping the knees straight.

Two   Lower heels to the foor.

Note: When lowering the heels to the floor, do not drop the weight of the body suddenly, as it will jar you. Slightly bending the knees as you lower the heels prevents any such jar.

*

†

‡

§

PREPARATION EXERCISE
PLIE (Plee-ay)

The French term "plie" means to bend; the Ballet term means to bend the knees, keeping heels on the floor, and extending the knees well out to the sides. "Grand Plie" means a deep bend, lowering the body as far as possible in the bend. A Half-plie" (or demi plie) is a slight bend.
Keep your back straight, your head up and the knees well out to the sides.

COUNTS
* ONE   Half-Plie
  Two   Return to Position
† Three   Grand Plie
  Four   Return to Position
* Five   Half-Plie
  Six   Return to Position
† Seven   Grand Plie
  Eight   Return to Position.

Repeat, practicing as many times as you need to feel that you have the correct interpretation of the terms.

BAR EXERCISE NUMBER ONE

Preparation:
Stand in FIRST POSITION, about 18 inches from the bar. Face LEFT. Lightly grasp the bar with the left hand, extending the right hand gracefully to the FRONT. The swing to the side in SECOND POSITION.
(This movement is to precede each exercise unless other preparation movement is given).

You are now in FIRST POSITION

COUNTS
ONE   Grand Plie. Swing right arm in low First Position
‡ { Two   Return to Position
    Three Grand Plie again
    Four Return to Position
FIVE   Relever
And   Return to Position
Six   Relever
And   Return to Position
§ { Seven Relever
And   Return to Position
Eight   Relever
And   Return to Position.

Change into SECOND POSITION and do the same exercise for eight counts.
Change into FIFTH POSITION and repeat the exercise for eight counts.
Begin each Bar exercise facing LEFT grasping the bar with the left hand going through preparatory movement gracefully, and then doing the exercise.
Then, make a complete turn, towards the Bar until you are facing RIGHT. Facing right, repeat the entire exercise, grasping the Bar with the right hand. This is to be done in every bar exercise.

LESSON FORTY-FIVE

EXERCISE NO. 2

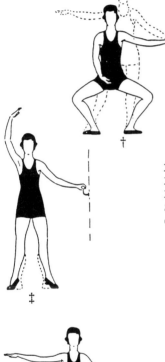

Before beginning a new exercise be sure that you are facing LEFT, grasping the bar with the left hand.

Stand in FIFTH POSITION. Extend arm into SECOND POSITION.

COUNTS

* ONE		Slide right foot to SIDE, pointing the toe and bending the arch as you touch foot to floor
	And	Slide foot back into FIFTH POSITION in BACK of left foot
* Two		Point right foot to SIDE
	And	Slide into FIFTH POSITION, right foot in FRONT of left.

Repeat this "petite battement" movement sixteen times, alternately siding the foot in FRONT and BACK of the left foot on the "and" counts.

This exercise is used to develop the ankles and to develop the arch of the foot. Unless done strenuously, the muscles do not get the value they should.

Retaining the same position as above, repeat the exercise as given to double time and do not touch the floor with toe when pointing to the SIDE. This movement is called "Frappe".

Repeat through sixteen counts. Then turn to RIGHT, grasping the bar with the right hand and do both exercises sixteen times.

EXERCISE NO. 3

Following the Petite Battement and the Plie and Relever Exercises, I will give you a combination of Petite Brush Battements and Half-Plies.

Stand in FIFTH POSITION. Grasp the bar with the left hand, extended arm in SECOND POSITION.

COUNTS

	ONE	Brush the right foot on floor in "battement" toe pointing to SIDE
	And	Return to FIFTH POSITION, right foot in FRONT of left
*	Two	Brush right foot, pointing to side in "battement"
	And	Return to FIFTH POSITION, right foot in BACK of left
† Three		Slide right foot into SECOND POSITION and a half-plie; half-plie does not require you to bend knees so far as does a grand plie.
Four		Slide back into FIFTH POSITION.

Repeat through counts "two and", then:

‡ Three		Slide right foot in SECOND POSITION and relever.

Make complete turn, grasping the bar with right and repeat the exercises.

Note: Let me remind you that the Ballet term "half-toe" means the ball of the foot, and "toe" means point of the toes. When dancing on the toes, toe slippers must be worn.

NED WAYBURN'S

COURSE IN STAGE DANCING

ACROBATIC HIGH KICKING ROUTINE
Medium 2/4 tempo

ENTRANCE STEP
8 measures

This step consists of four Hitch Kicks (back and front) advancing from stage LEFT to center stage.

Count

ONE   Swing right leg up behind

TWO   Swing left leg up behind and right leg down

THREE Swing left leg down and kick right leg FRONT (hip-high)

FOUR   Swing right leg down and do high kick with left leg.

Repeat three more times. On count "ONE" of each succeeding repetition, the left leg swings down from front kick and the right swings up behind.

* FIRST STEP
8 measures

Still facing stage RIGHT, do eight Control Kicks.

Count

ONE   High kick with right leg (A)
(1st meas.)

TWO   Hop on left and bend right knee,-(B) lowering right foot but holding thigh in place

THREE Hop on left foot and straighten right leg (A)

FOUR   Hop on left foot and bend right knee (B)
(2nd meas.)

Repeat these two measures for six more measures, lowering right leg on last count of the eighth measure.

† SECOND STEP
8 measures

Do eight high back kicks still travelling backward toward stage LEFT

Count

ONE   Back kick with right leg (B)
(1st meas.)

TWO   Hop on left foot, swinging right leg to floor (A)

Repeat for eight measures

♀ THIRD STEP
8 measures

The last movement brought the dancer to the stage LEFT and facing stage RIGHT. On measures 1-2-3, bend forward, placing palms of hands on floor and swing left leg up in back as high as possible, knee straight, head back (A)

1926 ...ce Masters of America routines. Copyright 1926 by Ned Wayburn Studios of Stage Dancing. Reproduced from the Dance Masters of America Collection, Dance Collection, The New York Public Library for the performing Arts.

Measures 4-5-6-7-8- Extend hands to side (second position) and keeping left leg in arabesque position; hop on right leg to each beat of the music, advancing to center stage.(B)

* FOURTH STEP

8 measures The dancer executes a pas de bourree to the LEFT and then a high left side kick; then the reverse to the RIGHT, always touching the toe at top of kick with the opposite hand.

Count

ONE Step right foot to LEFT OBLIQUE BACK

And Step left foot to LEFT

(1st meas.)

TWO Step right foot across in front of left

ONE Side kick left foot high to LEFT

(2nd meas.)

TWO Lower left foot toward floor

ONE Step left foot across in back of right foot

And Step right foot to RIGHT

(3rd meas.)

TWO Step left foot across in front of right foot

ONE Side kick right foot high to RIGHT

(4th meas.)

TWO Lower right foot toward floor

Repeat for four more measures

+ FIFTH STEP

8 measures The last step brought the dancer to stage center. Do a high side kick with the right leg, catching hold of the ankle at the top of kick with the left hand. Hop on each musical beat turning to each stage direction - RIGHT OBLIQUE, RIGHT, RIGHT OBLIQUE BACK, etc. - for the first four measures. Then reverse for the next four measures, turning to LEFT.

⸘ SIXTH STEP

8 measures

1st meas. Fan kick with left leg

2nd meas. Fan kick with right leg

3rd meas. Fan kick with left leg

4th meas. Fan kick with right leg

The next four measures are taken by Fan Kicks with the right leg.

+ EXIT STEP

8 measures

1st meas. Bring right knee against shoulder and, supporting it with right forearm, straighten knee and point

2nd meas. Then extend both arms into second position keeping right leg up •
For measures 3-4-5-6-7, hop on left foot, still keeping right leg in air

8th meas. On eighth measure, swing right leg down and in back, making a low curtsey.

"HEAH AH CUM"—Step 1, count 1   "HOW CUM"—Step 1, count 1   "PUSHIN' ROUND"—Step 2, count 3-4-5

The SAVANNAH STOMP

A Sensational Solo or Ensemble Number, by Ned Wayburn

Photographs of Beryl Halley, a Ned Wayburn Protegée, by Arthur Muray

Entrance Step—Face RIGHT (through 6 bars) 4 counts to each bar.

1 Step forward on ball of left foot, knee and toe pointed in.

2 Turn on ball of left foot so toe is straight; drop left heel hard.

3 Step forward on ball of right foot, knee and toe pointed in.

4 Turn on ball of right foot, toe straight; drop heel hard.

5 Step downstage on ball of left foot (long step) and bring right foot downstage alongside of left foot.

6 Step downstage on flat of left foot (short step).
NOTE: Counts 5 and 6 are done in two-step time.

7 Step upstage on ball of right foot; toe in.

8 Draw left foot upstage alongside of right foot; drop right heel hard.
Do not step on left foot.
Do the above three times.

Break

1 Step on ball of left foot; toe pointed in (short step).

2 Twist body to left; face downstage, turning on ball of left foot, and step downstage on ball of right foot.

3 Drop right heel hard.

4 ⎫
5 ⎬ Repeat movement, facing upstage.
6 ⎭

7 Stamp flat of left foot to face stage RIGHT again.

8 Stamp flat of Right Foot, facing RIGHT.
Repeat the entire two movements, end-

"DAT'S DAT"—Step 2, count 6

ing facing FRONT on count 7. DO NOT DO THE 8th COUNT. This covers sixteen bars of music—the first eight bars are the Entrance Step and the second eight cover the First Step.

Second Step—Start facing FRONT, hands on hips, thumbs forward, feet apart.

1 Sway to left, putting weight on left foot, keeping inner edge of right shoe on floor, right knee down, both knees bent.

2 Sway to right, reversing above position.

3-4 Repeat the above.

5 Step to LEFT OBLIQUE with left foot.

6 Brush right foot to LEFT OBLIQUE, turning left to face BACK, thrusting right foot downstage.

7 Drop left heel.

8 Step on right foot and draw left up to right toe.

1 Step on left toe.

2 Stamp left heel (keeping toe in place).

3-4-5 (Bend both knees, keeping weight on ball of left foot). Knees on same line, separated about 12 inches, hands on hips, leaning forward, push around to face FRONT with the right foot as though you had lumbago.

6 Raise right leg, knee bent, slap

knee with both hands, pushing foot down.

7 Stamp right foot on floor.

8 Rest.

REPEAT last fifteen counts.

Third Step—(Pick-up) Instead of resting on the 8th count the second time, do a pick-up.

And Stamp left foot LEFT.

A Stamp right foot alongside of left.

1 Stamp left foot to LEFT (knees bent).

2 Slide back on left foot, kick right foot to LEFT OBLIQUE (both knees bent).

3 Step on right foot to LEFT.

4 Step to LEFT on left foot (knees bent).

5 Slide back on left foot again, kicking right foot out.

6 Step on right foot to LEFT.

7 Step to LEFT on left foot.

8 Clap hands.

1 Slide back on left foot (kick right foot front).

And step LEFT OBLIQUE on right foot.

2 Rest.

3 Step LEFT OBLIQUE on left foot.

4 Step LEFT OBLIQUE on right foot.

5 Rest.

And Slide back on right foot (kick left foot to LEFT OBLIQUE).

6 Step LEFT OBLIQUE on left foot.

7 Step LEFT OBLIQUE on right foot.

Repeat from pick-up. On the "repeat," the last three counts are:—

And—Step down on left foot.

6—Step down on right foot.

7—Step down on left foot.

On this step make the "and—6" a slight jump, knock-kneed.

"PAS-MA-LAH"—*Step 3, count 1*

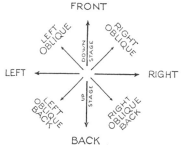

FRONT

LEFT OBLIQUE / RIGHT OBLIQUE

DOWN STAGE

LEFT ——— RIGHT

UP STAGE

LEFT OBLIQUE BACK / RIGHT OBLIQUE BACK

BACK

Use this diagram. Front is audience

Fourth Step

1 Cross right foot over left, stepping on the ball of foot.

2 Drop right heel.

3 Step back on left foot to RIGHT OBLIQUE BACK.

4 Hop on left foot, swinging right foot in a low circle to RIGHT OBLIQUE BACK.

5 Step on right foot.

6 Step back on left foot.

7 Step FRONT on right foot. } Two-

And Step front on left foot. } step.

8 Step front on right foot.

1 Cross left foot over right, stepping on ball of left.

2 Slide back to RIGHT OBLIQUE BACK on left foot, raising right in air back.

3 Step on right foot.

4 Cross left foot over right and step again.

5 Slide back on left foot again.

6 Step on right foot again.

7 Stamp on left foot to LEFT OBLIQUE ...

8 Rest.

Repeat this step sixteen counts.

*T*HE *Savannah Stomp embodies all the verve and joyous spirit of the Jazz Age, permitting a fascinating abandon in its execution. It may be effectively used as a specialty solo, or as an ensemble number.*

THE EDITOR

"... FLY"—*Step 3, count 7*

"SWINGING WIDE"—*Step 4, count 3*

"TARIN' ROUND"—*Step 4, count 4*

AMPICO RECORDING

207331F Ned Wayburn's Original Charleston

HOW TO DANCE

NED WAYBURN'S
BALLROOM CHARLESTON

The "Charleston" we are about to learn is a smooth and graceful ballroom dance based on the movements of the stage Charleston which I was first to present to the public in the Follies of 1923 and have since been teaching in the NED WAYBURN STUDIOS both as a stage and a ballroom dance.

Ned Wayburn
1926

NED WAYBURN'S
ORIGINAL BALLROOM CHARLESTON

Before going into the dance itself let me call your attention to Figure A. It is a diagram* of the eight stage directions I have always used in training my stars and choruses in large productions as well as the many exhibition ballroom dancing teams who have sought my assistance. Become familiar with these directions, as they will be used throughout the following practice steps and in the dance itself.

Next comes a word about tempo. Again I must revert to my system of teaching stage dances as the clearest and most simple method of counting. Play the Ampico Charleston recording through and count aloud - "and one," "and two," etc., as printed on the recording, to the music.

I would suggest setting the tempo indicator at sixty for the practice of all of the steps until you are thoroughly familiar with each movement. When you are ready to try the dance with a partner set the indicator at seventy-five. At this speed you will be able to do the dance comfortably and with sufficient time to perfect yourself. When you have perfected the dance, do it with the indicator at one hundred which is the correct tempo for the ballroom Charleston.

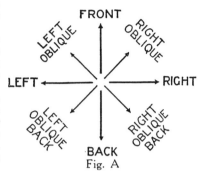

Fig. A

The lady and gentleman stand in the ballroom position about nine inches apart. The gentleman's part is described throughout, the lady doing exactly the opposite, such as when we say gentleman "left foot forward" the lady will put her right foot back, when the gentleman moves to right, the lady will move to left, etc.

Characteristic Time Step Of
Ballroom Charleston

Characteristic Step Practice

Stand on both feet weight evenly distributed, feet three inches apart. Try the ankle movement: on the count of "and", shift the weight on the left foot turn the heel of the right foot out, the ball of the right foot remaining on the floor. On the count of "one" return the right foot flat on the floor. (See illustration No. 1). Repeat this movement seven times. (The "and" count being the action count of the heel turning out). On the eighth count shift the weight to the balls of both feet and turn both heels out. (Illustration No. 2). During this movement the knee should be bent in on the count of "and". Repeat the same movement on the next seven counts, shifting the weight to the right foot, turning the left heel out leaving the ball of the left foot on the floor. (Illustration No. 3). Repeat the entire movement twice. This will give the desired ankle effect.

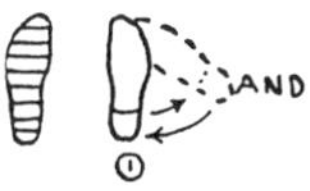

Fig. 1

Fig. 2

Fig. 3

Forward and Backward Movement of Characteristic Step

On the count of "and" the left knee is slightly bent, left heel raised off floor, toes turned in. On the count of "one" the left foot is pointed forward touching the floor, the weight being on the right foot. On the count of "and" the left foot is raised and count "two" brought back to the starting position. On the count of "and" the right knee is bent and the weight is shifted to the left foot, right heel raised off floor, toes turned in. On the count of "three" right foot pointed to the back. The right knee is bent on "four", the foot is brought back to the starting point. (Illustration No. 4). On the "and" counts one foot will be raised with the knee bent, while the other foot will carry the weight, the heel being turned out. After you have learned the forward and backward movement as on illustration No. 4, proceed with dance - note on each "and" count use the character ankle movement on the foot bearing the weight, as in illustration No. 5.

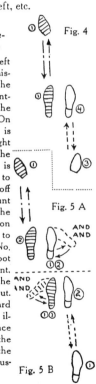

Fig. 4

Fig. 5 A

Fig. 5 B

The Dance Begins - 1st Step

The gentleman steps the left foot 18 inches forward, the lady, the right foot back, taking four walking steps, the gentleman going forward. (Illustration 6A). On the fourth walking step the weight is shifted to the right foot. On the count of "and" the left knee is bent up and goes into the character Charleston step with the left foot forward. The character forward and backward movement repeat three times, or twelve counts. (Illustration 6B).

The Figure 8 Step, Left

The movement is now repeated on the opposite side, stepping out with the left foot, as in illustration 7B. On the count of "one" the left foot steps forward. On the count of "two" right foot passes across in front to the left about eight inches apart. On the count of "three" left foot goes directly left passing behind right. On the count of "four" the right foot steps left oblique back. On the count of "five" left foot passes back of the right foot, right oblique back, on the count of "six" the right foot goes to the right, on the count of "seven" left foot passes behind the right going to the right, on the count of "eight" the right foot steps forward to starting position. This completes the figure "eight" step.

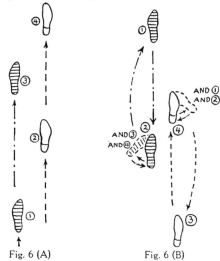

Fig. 6 (A)   Fig. 6 (B)

The Figure "Eight" Step, Right - 2nd Step

On the count of "one" the gentleman steps the left foot forward, on the count of "two" step right foot, right oblique, on the count of "three" the left foot passes in front of the right foot going to the right about eight inches, on the count of "four" the right foot goes right oblique back, on the count of "five", the left foot steps back, on the count of "six" the right foot crosses the back of left foot going left oblique back (eight inches apart), on the count of "seven" the left foot goes directly left, on the count of "eight" right foot back to starting position. (Illustration 7A).

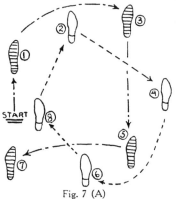

Fig. 7 (A)

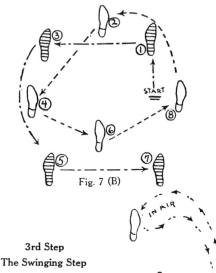

Fig. 7 (B)

3rd Step
The Swinging Step

Next the Swinging Step. Step left oblique on the left foot for the count of "one." Swing the right foot, in the air, left oblique for the "two" count (do not touch the floor) Step right oblique back for the "three" count. Swing the left foot, in the air, right oblique back for the "four" count. Repeat the movement four times ending with the left foot in the air, right oblique back. (Illustration 8)

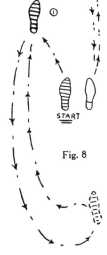

Fig. 8

4th Step
Charleston Polka

On the count of "one" step left foot 18 inches to left. On count of "and" draw right foot beside it. On the count of "two" step left foot to left 18 inches. On the count of "and" touch the floor with the toe of the right foot in the place it has been, knee turned in toward left foot. On the count of "three" touch the heel. On the count of "and" touch the toe· On the count of "four" touch the heel, on the count of "and" the toe again. (Illustration 9 A.)

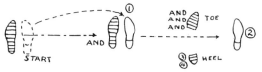

Fig. 9 [A]

On the count of "one" put the weight on the right foot, on the count of "and" draw the left foot to it, on the count of "two" step right foot to right 18 inches, on the count of "and" strike the floor with the toe of the left foot in the position it has been, knee turned in towards left foot, on the count of "three" strike the floor with the heel of the left foot, on the count of "and" with the toe of the left foot, on the count of "four" with the heel, on the count of "and" with the toe. This movement is done twice. (Illustration 9 B.)

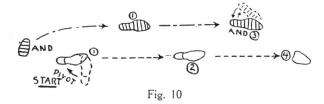

Fig. 9 [B]

This dance thus far is the complete first chorus of the music. Coming out of the Charleston Polka the toe of the left foot is still on the floor on the count of "and". On the count of "one" pivot on the ball of the right foot facing right and take one step forward with the left foot. On the count of "two" step forward on right foot, on the count of "three" stepforward on the left foot. On the count of "and" do the character ankle movement with the left foot, and on the count of "four" point the right foot forward. (Illustration 10).

Fig. 10

NED WAYBURN
Studios of Stage Dancing Inc.

1841 Broadway,(Entr.on 60th St.)Studio 000,
At Columbus Circle,New York. Open all year 'round
9 A. M. to 10 P. M. Except Sundays.
(Closed Saturdays at 6 P. M.) Phone Columbus 3500

The Original "**Footloose**" Strut

Dance Sensation of the Year

BY

NED WAYBURN

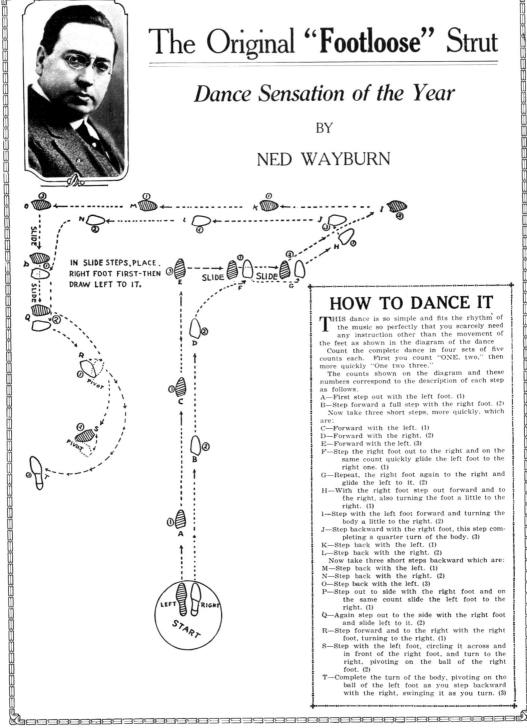

IN SLIDE STEPS, PLACE.
RIGHT FOOT FIRST—THEN
DRAW LEFT TO IT.

HOW TO DANCE IT

THIS dance is so simple and fits the rhythm of the music so perfectly that you scarcely need any instruction other than the movement of the feet as shown in the diagram of the dance

Count the complete dance in four sets of five counts each. First you count "ONE, two," then more quickly "One two three."

The counts shown on the diagram and these numbers correspond to the description of each step as follows.

A—First step out with the left foot. (1)

B—Step forward a full step with the right foot. (2)

Now take three short steps, more quickly, which are:

C—Forward with the left. (1)

D—Forward with the right. (2)

E—Forward with the left. (3)

F—Step the right foot out to the right and on the same count quickly glide the left foot to the right one. (1)

G—Repeat, the right foot again to the right and glide the left to it. (2)

H—With the right foot step out forward and to the right, also turning the foot a little to the right. (1)

I—Step with the left foot forward and turning the body a little to the right. (2)

J—Step backward with the right foot, this step completing a quarter turn of the body. (3)

K—Step back with the left. (1)

L—Step back with the right. (2)

Now take three short steps backward which are:

M—Step back with the left. (1)

N—Step back with the right. (2)

O—Step back with the left. (3)

P—Step out to side with the right foot and on the same count slide the left foot to the right. (1)

Q—Again step out to the side with the right foot and slide left to it. (2)

R—Step forward and to the right with the right foot, turning to the right. (1)

S—Step with the left foot, circling it across and in front of the right foot, and turn to the right, pivoting on the ball of the right foot. (2)

T—Complete the turn of the body, pivoting on the ball of the left foot as you step backward with the right, swinging it as you turn. (3)

ZIMMERMAN PRINT. CINCINNATI

Books

Astaire, Fred. *Steps in Time*. New York: Harper, 1959.

Baral, Robert. *Revue: A Nostalgic Reprise of the Great Broadway Period*. New York: Fleet Publishing, 1962.

Blesh, Rudi, and Harriet Janis. *They All Played Ragtime: The True Story of an American Music*. New York: Knopf, 1950.

Blumenthal, George (as told to Arthur H. Menkin). *My 60 Years in Show Business*. New York: Frederick C. Osberg, 1936.

Botkin, B.A., ed. *New York City Folklore*. New York: Random House, 1956.

Cantor, Eddie, with Jane Kesner Ardmore. *Take My Life*. Garden City, N.Y.: Doubleday, 1957.

Cantor, Eddie, and David Friedman. *Ziegfeld: The Great Glorifier*. New York: Alfred H. King, 1934.

Carter, Randolph. *The World of Flo Ziegfeld*. New York: Praeger, 1934.

Castle, Irene. *Castles in the Air*. Garden City, N.Y.: Doubleday, 1958.

Charters, Ann. *Nobody: The Story of Bert Williams*. New York: Macmillan, 1970.

Cohan, George M. *Twenty Years on Broadway and the Years It Took to Get There*. New York: Harper, 1925.

de Courville, Albert. *I Tell You*. London: Chapman and Hall, 1928.

Dumont, Frank. *The Witmark Amateur Minstrel Guide and Burnt Cork Encyclopedia*. Chicago and New York: M. Witmark and Sons, 1899.

Emerson, Nathaniel B. *Unwritten Literature of Hawaii*. Rutland, Vt.: Charles E. Tuttle Co., 1965. This was written in 1909 for the United States Bureau of American Ethnology.

Ewen, David. *Great Men of American Popular Song*. Englewood Cliffs, N.J.: Prentice-Hall, 1972.

Gammond, Peter. *Scott Joplin and the Ragtime Era*. New York: St. Martin's Press, 1975.

Gershwin, Ira. *Lyrics on Several Occasions*. New York: Viking, 1973.

Gilbert, Douglas. *American Vaudeville: Its Life and Times*. New York: Dover, 1968.

Higham, Charles. *Ziegfeld*. Chicago: Henry Regnery Co., 1972.

Irwin, Inez Hayes. *The Story of the Women's Party*. New York: Harcourt Brace, 1921.

Jablonski, Edward, and Lawrence D. Stewart. *The Gershwin Years*. Garden City, N.Y.: Doubleday, 1958.

Jasen, David A. *Recorded Ragtime: 1897–1958*. Hamdon, Conn.: Archon Books/Shoe String Press, 1973.

Johanssen, Albert. *The House of Beadle and Adams and its Dime and Nickel Novels*. Norman, Okla.: University of Oklahoma Press, 1950.

Kendall, Elizabeth. *Where She Danced*. New York: Knopf, 1979.

Money, Keith. *Anna Pavlova: Her Life and Art*. New York: Knopf, 1982.

Morehouse, Ward. *George M. Cohan: Prince of the American Theatre*. Philadelphia and New York: J.P. Lippincott Co., 1943.

Morgan, Anna. *An Hour with Delsarte*. Boston: Lee and Sherman, 1895.

O'Brien, Frederick. *Mystic Isles of the South Seas*. New York: Century Co., 1921.

_____. *White Shadows of the South Seas*. New York: Century Co., 1919.

Phillips, Clarence Coles. *A Gallery of Girls*. New York: Life Publishing Co., [1912].

_____. *The Phillips Calendar*. New York: Life Publishing Co., 1912.

Ruyter, Nancy Lee Chalfa. *Reformers and Visionaries: The Americanization of the Art of Dance*. New York: Dance Horizons, 1980.

Schaefer, William J., and Johannes Reidel. *The Art of Ragtime: Form and Meaning of an Original Black American Art*. Baton Rouge, La.: Louisiana State University Press, 1973.

Stearns, Marshall and Jean. *Jazz Dance: The Story of American Vernacular Dance*. New York: Macmillan, 1964; rpt., New York: DaCapo, 1994.

Stebbins, Genevieve. *The Delsarte System of Expression*. New York: Edgar S. Werner, 1883.

_____. *Society Gymnastics and Voice Culture*. New York: Edgar S. Werner, 1888.

Wayburn, Ned. *The Art of Stage Dancing*. New York: Ned Wayburn Studios of Stage Dancing, 1925, 1927.

West, Mae. *Goodness Had Nothing to Do With It*. Englewood Cliffs, N.J.: Prentice-Hall, 1956.

Wilder, Alec. *American Popular Song: The Great Innovators, 1900–1950*. New York: Oxford University Press, 1972.

Wilbor, Elsie M., ed. *The Delsarte Recitation Book*. New York: Edgar S. Werner, 1888, 1893.

Wittke, Carl. *Tambo and Bones*. Durham, N.C.: Duke University Press, 1930.

Dance Instruction Manuals

Albertieri, Luigi. *The Art of Terpsichore*. New York: C. Ricordi and Co., 1923.

Baron, Samuel. *Professor Baron's Complete Instructor in All the Society Dances of America*. New York: M. Young, 1881.

Blasis, Carlo. *An Elementary Treatise Upon the Theory and Practise of the Art of Dancing*. Trans. Mary Stewart Evans. New York: Kamin Dance Publishers, 1944; rpt., New York: Dover, 1968.

Butler, Albert and Josephine. "Encyclopedia of Social Dance." New York: Albert and Josephine Butler, 1975. Typescript in the Dance Collection, New York Public Library for the Performing Arts.

Castle, Vernon and Irene. *Modern Dancing*. New York: World Syndicate Co., 1914.

Cellarius, Henri. *The Drawing-Room Dances*. London: E. Churton Publishers, 1847.

_____. *The Social Dances of the Salon*. New York: Dinsmore and Co., 1858. Pirated edition of *The Drawing-Room Dances*.

Chalif, Louis H. *The Chalif Text Books of Dancing*. 5 vols. New York: Chalif Normal School of Dancing, 1918–1925.

Clendenen, F. Leslie. *The Art of Dancing*. St. Louis, Mo.: Leslie F. Clendenen, 1919.

_____. *Dance Mad, or The Dances of the Day*. St. Louis, Mo.: Arcade Print Co., 1914.

_____. *Quadrille Book*. Chicago: Chart Music Publishing House, 1899.

Cleveland, C.H., Jr. *Dancing at Home and Abroad*. Boston: Oliver Ditson and Co., 1878.

Craske, Margaret, and Cyril W. Beaumont. *The Theory and Practise of Allegro in Classical Ballet (Cecchetti Method)*. London: C.W. Beaumont, 1930.

Crozier, Gladys. *The Tango and How To Do It*. London: Andrew Melrose, 1913.

Dancing Without a Master. Philadelphia: Royal Publishing Co., 1917.

Dick's Quadrille Call Book and Ball-Room Prompter. New York: Dick and Fitzgerald Publishers, 1895.

Dodworth, Allen. *Dancing and Its Relations to Education and Social Life*. London and New York: Harper, 1885, 1905.

Duryea, Oscar. "Lessons in Fancy Dancing." *The World Magazine*, 10 Feb. 1912, p. 10.

Enebuske, Claës J. *Progressive Gymnastic Day's Order According to the Principles of the Ling System*. New York: Silver, Burdett and Co., 1892.

Fancy Drills for Evening and Other Entertainments. London and New York: Butterick Publishing Co., 1894.

Forrester, Francis. *Minnie's Playroom, or How to Practise Calisthenics*. Boston: George C. Rand, 1854.

The German: How to Give It, How to Lead It, How to Dance It, by Two Amateur Leaders. Chicago: A.C. McClurg and Co., 1890, 1897.

Hartelius, Prof. T. J. *Home Gymnastics*. Trans. C. Löfring. Philadelphia: J.P. Lippincott Co., 1896.

Hopkins, J. S. *The Tango and Other Up-to-date Dances*. Chicago: Saalfield Publishing Co., 1914.

Hostetler, Lawrence A. *The Art of Social Dancing*. New York: A.S. Barnes and Co., 1930.

Keeling, John Gilbert. *The Art of Acrobatic Dancing*. Oklahoma City, Okla.: Halbert R. Stephens, 1929.

Kinney, Troy, and Margaret West. *Social Dancing of Today*. New York: Frederick A. Stokes Co., 1914. The dances were demonstrated for this book by John Murray Anderson.

Kosloff, Alexis. *Russian Ballet Technique*. New York: Alexis Kosloff, 1921.

Lussan-Borel. *Traité de Danse*. Paris: Albin Michel, 1914.

McClow, Lloyd L. *Tumbling Illustrated*. New York: Lloyd L. McClow, 1931.

Marinoff, Sergei [pseud.]. *A Manual of Classic Dancing: Exercises and Practises for the Development of the Classic Dancer*. 3rd. ed. Chicago: Sergei Martinoff School of Classic Dancing, 1924. This was the bound volume of "The Sergei Marinoff Home-Study Course of Classic Dancing, 1923–1924."

Middleton, Elizabeth Avis. *Scarf Fantastics*. New York: Edgar S. Werner, 1896.

Morton, Marguerite W. *Ideal Drills*. Philadelphia: Penn Publishing Co., 1926. Includes material copyrighted between 1893 and 1924.

Newman, Albert W. *Newman Album of Classical Dances*. Philadelphia: Theodore Presser Co., 1923.

Nissen, Hartvig. *The ABC of the Swedish System of Educational Gymnastics*. Philadelphia: F.A. Davis, 1891.

Norman, Frank. *The Scarf Dance and Tableau*. Buffalo, N.Y.: Two-Step Publishing Co., 1919.

Peters, Prof. A. *Des Leçons de Danse: le Shimmy et la Java*. Paris: Editions Nilsson, 1920.

Posse, Baron Nils M.G. *Modern Gymnastics*. Paris: Pierre Lafitte et Cie., 1913.

Rivera, Max. *Le Tango et les Danses Nouvelles*. Boston: Lothrop, Lee and Shepard, 1890.

Rivers, Charles H. *The Dancing Tablet*. Brooklyn, N.Y.: Charles H. Rivers, 1897.

Tarasoff, Ivan. "Dance Your Way to Slenderness." *Dance Lovers Magazine*, Dec. 1924, pp. 14–15, 62; Jan. 1925, pp. 27, 59; Feb. 1925, pp. 28–29, 68.

Walker, H. Layton. *Twentieth Century Cotillion Figures*. Buffalo, N.Y.: Two-Step Publishing Co., 1912.

Wayburn, Ned. "How to Take Care of Your Feet." *Dance Lovers Magazine*, Aug. 1925, pp. 14–15.

_____. *Ned Wayburn's Health and Beauty Course*. New York: Ned Wayburn Studios of Stage Dancing, 1927, 1932.

_____. "The Hitch Kick." *Dance Lovers Magazine*, May 1924, p. 56.

_____. "The Savannah Stomp." *The Dance Magazine*, Mar. 1928, pp. 18–19.

Zorn, Frederich Albert. *The Grammar of the Art of Dancing*. New York: Burt Franklyn, 1970.

Unpublished Manuals

Dance Masters of America, Inc. Descriptions of dances as taught at Annual Conventions and Normal Schools, 1926–1941. Vols. 1–2 (Oscar Duryea), 3–4 (Ernest Belcher, Chester Hale), 9–10 (Ivan Tarasoff), 11–12 (social dances), and 15 (Ned Wayburn). Materials donated to the Dance Collection, New York Public Library for the Performing Arts, by Catherine B. Sullivan.

Instructions for dances and individual steps published in the following periodicals: *The American Dancer, The Dance, Dance Culture Magazine, Dance Lovers Magazine, The Dance Magazine, Dance Review, The Director, The Modern Dance Magazine* (two different magazines of this name), *Physical Culture Magazine*, and *The Terpsichorean* (after 1913, *The Two-Step*).

The following works were in the research and discussion phase during the original writing of this monograph but were published after the bibliography was finalized:

Johnson, Stephen Burge. *The Roof Gardens of Broadway Theatres, 1883–1942*. Ann Arbor, Mich.: UMI Research Press, 1985.

Malnig, Julie. *Dancing Till Dawn: A Century of Exhibition Ballroom Dance*. New York: Greenwood Press, 1992.

Maschio, Geraldine. "The *Ziegfeld Follies*: Form, Content and Significance of an American Revue." Ph.D. diss., University of Wisconsin at Madison, 1981.

Musical Theatre in America: Papers and Proceedings of the Conference on the Music Theatre in America. Ed. Glenn Loney. Westport, Conn.: Greenwood Press, 1984. This conference was sponsored jointly by the American Society for Theatre Research, the Sonneck Society, and the Theatre Library Association.

Unpublished Theses

Curry, Wade Chester. "Steele MacKaye: Producer and Director." Ph.D. diss., University of Illinois, 1958.

Dillport, Rayda Walker. "The Pupils of François Delsarte." M.A. thesis, Louisiana State University, 1946.

Morris, Virginia Elizabeth. "The Influences of Delsarte in America as Revealed through the Lectures of Steele MacKaye." M.A. thesis, Louisiana State University, 1941.

Pamphlets

MacKaye, Steele. *François Delsarte, The Philosophy of Emotion and its Expression in Art.* New York: John F. Trow and Son, 1875.

Wayburn, Ned. *Your Career: How to Win Health, Beauty and Independence.* New York: Ned Wayburn Institute of Dancing, 1931.

Articles and Monographs

Many of the articles listed below were published in periodicals that did not use volume or series numerations. In order to make the listing consistent, I have eliminated volume and series numbers for all articles.

Please note that the periodical entitled *The Dance Magazine* between 1925 and ca. 1931 is not the same publication as *Dance Magazine*; the latter, then called *The American Dancer*, was published in this period on the West Coast and covered dance activity in this region.

Austin, Fred. "The Modern Dancing Masters." *The Dance Magazine*, Sept. 1926, pp. 20–21, 59.

Baker, Colgate. "Mr. Wayburn says..." *The New York Review*, 20 July 1912, n.p.

Baldwin, Sidney. "The History of the Wayburn Schools." *Dance Lovers Magazine*, Feb. 1925, pp. 15–16.

Barzel, Ann. "European Dance Teachers in the United States." *Dance Index*, Apr.–June 1944.

Bie, Oscar. "Europe's Latest Fad: Modern Stage Dancing." *The Musical Courier*, 15 July 1920, pp. 6–7.

Carroll, Earl. "Making a Song Hit." *The Music Trade*, 9 Dec. 1911, n.p.

Caspary, Vera. "What is a Good Kick Worth?" *Dance Lovers Magazine*, Sept. 1924, pp. 20–21, 61.

Cather, Willa. "Training for the Ballet." *McClures Magazine*, Oct. 1913, p. 90.

Clayton, Bessie. "The Language of the Feet." *Green Book*, Dec. 1931, pp. 233–234.

Cohen, Barbara Naomi. "Ballet Satire in the Early Broadway Revue." *Dance Scope* (Winter-Spring 1979), pp. 44–50.

_____. "The Borrowed Art of Gertrude Hoffmann." *Dance Data No. 2* (1977), pp. 2–11.

_____. "Chain Prologs: Dance at the Picture Palaces." *Dance Scope* (Fall 1978), pp. 12–23.

_____. "Fancy Dancing and Tap and Stepping." *Dance Scope* (Winter 1980), pp. 34–47.

_____. "Modern Americanized Ballet: 'Her Stage of Perpetual Chiffon.'" *Dance Scope* (Spring 1980), pp. 25–35.

Cooper, H.E. "A Cycle of Dance Crazes: The Houchi-couchi, Cakewalk and Charleston are Birds of a Feather that now Find a Warm Nest in the Revue." *The Dance Magazine*, Feb. 1927, pp. 28–29, 50.

_____. "Glorifying the American Leg: Concerning the Chorus and its Rise to Respectability." *The Dance Magazine*, Mar. 1927, pp. 26–27, 57.

_____. "Variety, Vaudeville and Virtue." *The Dance Magazine*, Dec. 1927, pp. 31–32.

[Cooper, H.E.]. "Beauty, Talent, or What have you?" *The Dance Magazine*, Feb. 1927, pp. 11–12, 52.

Erenberg, Lewis A. "Everybody's Doing It: The Pre-World War I Dance Craze, the Castles and the Modern American Girl." *Feminist Studies* (Fall 1975), pp. 155–170.

Gaye, Pamela. "The Legacy of the Minstrel Show." *Dance Scope* (Spring-Summer 1978), pp. 34–45.

Hardy, Camille. "Bessie Clayton: An American Genée." *Dance Chronicle* (1978–1979), pp. 251–278.

Kaye, Joseph. "Master of the 'Follies': Florenz Ziegfeld, Jr." *The Dance Magazine*, Oct. 1929, pp. 15–17, 58–59; Nov. 1929, pp. 18–20, 55, 57; Dec. 1929, pp. 32–34, 54; Jan. 1930, pp. 40–42, 63.

Morgan, Mary. "Handling Humanity in the Masses." *The Theatre Magazine*, May 1913, pp. 146–147.

Mulvaney, Joseph. "The Tireless Tillers." *The Dance Magazine*, June 1926, pp. 22–23, 61.

Nathan, George Jean. "The Musical Show's Dependence on Girls." *Smart Set*, Oct. 1913, pp. 124–152.

O'Neill, Rosetta. "The Dodworth Family and Ballroom Dancing in New York." *Dance Index* (Apr. 1943), pp. 44–56.

Patterson, Ada. "Ned Wayburn." *The Theatre Magazine*, Dec. 1923, p. 22.

Pearson, E.L. "The Beadle Collection." *The Bulletin of The New York Public Library* (July 1922), pp. 550–629.

Pennington, Ann. "How Dancing Builds Sex Appeal." *The Dance Magazine*, Feb. 1928, pp. 10–11, 62.

Rock, William. "Stage Dancing as an Art." *Green Book*, July 1911, pp. 200–205.

Still, William Raymond. "A Quiet Day with Lew Fields and Ned Wayburn, or Leading the Simple Life." *The New York Review*, 10 Oct. 1909, n.p.

_____. "Teaching Lew Fields to Sing, or What's the Use." *The New York Review*, 17 Oct. 1909, n.p.

Wayburn, Ned. "Chorus Girls in the Making." *Green Book*, Oct. 1913, pp. 575–579.

_____. "'Realizing' Musical Shows." Unidentified periodical, 9 Feb. 1913, pp. 176–177.

_____. "Show Girls: Yesterday and Today." *The Theater Magazine*, Dec. 1916, pp. 362–363, 408.

_____. "The Stage Producer's Job." Unidentified periodical, c. 1912, pp. 801–809.

_____. "You Have Got to Have Legs." *Midnight*, Nov. 1922, pp. 7–8, 18.

Wayburn, Ned (as told to Byrne MacFadden). "Correct Dieting for Dancers." *Dance Lovers Magazine*, Nov. 1924, pp. 12, 65.

White, George (as told to Byrne MacFadden). "Musical Comedy Dancing." *The Dance Magazine*, Nov. 1925, pp. 32–33, 54.

White, George, and Nanette Kutner. "The Songs and Dance Game." *The Dance Magazine*, Jan. 1927, pp. 15–17, 52.

Ziegfeld, Florenz, Jr. "How I Pick My Stage Beauties." Newspaper Feature Service, ca. Oct. 1924.

———. "When is a Woman's Figure Beautiful?" Newspaper Feature Service, ca. Dec. 1922.

———. "Why Follies' Girls are Beautiful." *Strength Magazine*, Oct. 1924, n.p.

Scrapbooks

Patten Scrapbook of Photographs. Vol. 1. Dance Collection, New York Public Library for the Performing Arts.

Sol Bloom Scrapbook. Sol Bloom Collection, Box 49. Rare Books and Manuscript Division, New York Public Library.

Robinson Locke Collection Scrapbooks.* Billy Rose Theater Collection, New York Public Library for the Performing Arts:

Carroll, Earl (ser. 2); Carus, Emma (ser. 2); Castle, Irene Foote and Vernon (ser. 1); Ceballos, Hilarion and Rosalia (ser. 2); Clayton, Bessie (ser. 3); Conway, Hart (ser. 3); Cross and Josephine (ser. 3); De Haven and Nice (Grey Locke envelope); Dolores (ser. 2); Deslys, Gaby (ser. 1); Deslys, Gaby (ser. 2); Dolly, Jansczi and Roszika (ser. 2); Dolly, Jansczi and Roszika (ser. 3); Donahue, Jack (ser. 2); Eaton, Mary (ser. 2); Evans, Arthur R. (ser. 2); Fairbanks, Madeleine and Marion (listed as Thankhauser Twins, ser. 2); Falk, Eleanor (Grey Locke envelope); Faust, Lotte (ser. 2); Fields, Lew (ser. 2); Friganza, Trixie (ser. 2); Greenwood, Charlotte (Grey Locke envelope); Haig, Emma (Grey Locke envelope); Hammerstein, Oscar and William (ser. 1); Hawman, Elizabeth, Louise, and Margaret (Grey Locke envelope); Herron, Bertie (ser. 2); Hoffmann, Gertrude (ser. 1); Jennery, Trixie (Grey Locke envelope); King, Mazie (Grey Locke envelope); Liddell, Beatrice (Grey Locke envelope); Lorriane, Lillian (ser. 2); McNeil, Seppie (Grey Locke envelope); Moore, Gladys (ser. 3); Nice, Fred, Jr. (Grey Locke envelope); Nichols, Nellie V. (Grey Locke envelope); Pilcer, Harry (Grey Locke envelope); Ring, Blanche (ser. 3); Schaall, Ida (Grey Locke envelope); Warfield, David (ser. 2); Wayburn, Helen Davis (Grey Locke envelope); Wayburn, Ned (Grey Locke envelope); Wood, Swan (Grey Locke envelope); Zitelka, Dolores (ser. 2).

Personal and professional scrapbooks housed in the Billy Rose Theater Collection, New York Public Library for the Performing Arts:

Adelaide and Hughes (1 vol.); Atteridge, Harold (2 vols.); Boley, May (1 vol.); Capitol Theater, New York (5 vols. concerning Wayburn); Chicot (Epes Winthrop Sargeant) (3 vols. concerning Wayburn); Chorus (1 vol.); Cross and Josephine (1 vol.); Dickson, Dorothy (1 vol.); Dickson, Dorothy (1 vol.); Dixon, Harland (1 vol. concerning Wayburn); Gray, Gilda (1 vol.); Hardy, Sam B. (1 vol.); Kelety, Julia (1 vol.); Law, Evelyn (1 vol. of photographs, 2 vols. of clippings); Lean, Cecil (1 vol.); Lorraine, Lillian (1 vol.); McDonald, Donald (2 vols.); Minstrels, U.S., 19th-century (1 vol.); Shaw, Oscar (1 vol.); Vaudeville, U.S., acts (2 vols.); Wayburn, Ned (21 vols.); Wayburn Ned (1 vol.); Wheaton, Anna (1 vol.); White, George (1 vol.).

Clipping, Production, and Personality Files

This monograph has made great use of clipping, production, and personality files on individuals, shows, and theaters. These files include reviews, promotional articles, interviews, programs, and iconographic material. They are housed in the following collections:

Art and Architecture Division, New York Public Library.
Billy Rose Theater Collection, New York Public Library for the Performing Arts.
Dance Collection, New York Public Library for the Performing Arts.
Harvard Theater Collection, Harvard University Library.
Theater and Music Collection, Museum of the City of New York.
Music Division, New York Public Library for the Performing Arts.

Selected Manuscript Collections

MacKaye Family Papers, Baker Library, Dartmouth College Library.
Joseph Urban Papers. Boxes 5, 21, 36, 37, 38, 39, and 40 ("Production Materials"). Rare Books and Manuscripts, Butler Library, Columbia University.

Selected Interviews

Astaire, Fred. Telephone interview. Beverly Hills, Calif., 6 Dec. 1978.
Bartosh, Carole Paynter. Los Angeles, Calif., 8 Dec. 1978.
Hale, Chester. Redondo Beach, Calif., 14 Dec. 1976.
O'Denishawn, Florence. New York, N.Y., 8 Jan. 1979.
Otero-Friedman, Nona. Telephone interview. New York, N.Y., 25 Oct. 1978.
Vinton, Doris. New York, N.Y., 20 Oct. 1978.
Waldron, Harriet Fowler. Telephone interview. New York, N.Y., 30 Oct. 1978.
Weyburn, Edward Claudius, Jr. New York, N.Y., 27 Nov. 1979.

Song Listing

The songs below are listed in alphabetical order by title using the format adopted by Alec Wilder in his *American Popular Song: The Great Innovators* (1972). The following abbreviations are used for the collection sources:

BU – Sheet Music Collection, John Hay Library, Brown University, Providence, R.I.
CO – Office of Copyright Searches, United States Copyright Office, Crystal City, Md.
LC – Music Division, Library of Congress, Washington, DC.
MCNY – Theater and Music Collection, Museum of the City of New York (organized by show title).
MD – Special Collections, Music Division, New York Public Library for the Performing Arts (organized by song title).
MD-P.I. – Special Collections, Music Division, New York Public Library for the Performing Arts (organized by song title and arranger).
MD-U.C. – Special Collections, Music Division, New York Public Library for the Performing Arts (organized by year of publication and song title).

"A Pretty Girl is Like a Melody." Lyrics and music by Irving Berlin. Pub. Irving Berlin Music Publishing Co., 1919. *Ziegfeld Follies of 1919*. MCNY.

"After the Ball was Over." Lyrics by Arthur J. Jackson. Music by B. D. deSylva. Pub. Jerome H. Remick Co., 1918. *Ziegfeld Follies of 1918*. MD.

"Ain't It Funny What a Difference Just a Few Drinks Make." Lyrics by Gene Buck. Music by Jerome Kern. Pub. T. B. Harms Co., 1916. *Ziegfeld Follies of 1916*. LC.

"All the World is Dancing." Lyrics by Harold Atteridge. Music by Louis A. Hirsch. Pub. Shapiro Music Publishing Co., 1912. *Passing Show of 1912*. Copyright protection copy. Shubert Archive.

"Argentina." Lyrics by George E. Stoddard and Ned Wayburn. Music by Harold Orlob. Pub. T. B. Harms Co., 1921. *Passing Show of 1912*. LC.

"The Bacchanale Rag." Lyrics and music by Louis A. Hirsch. Pub. Shapiro Music Publishing Co., 1912. *Passing Show of 1912*. LC.

"Becky from Babylon." Lyrics by Alex Gerber. Music by Abner Silver. Pub. M. Witmark and Sons, 1920. Personal Collection.

"Becky is Back in the Ballet." Lyrics by Blanche Merrill. Music by Leo Edwards. Pub. M. Witmark and Sons, 1921. Personal Collection.

"Big Chief Battle Axe." Lyrics and music by Thomas S. Allen. Pub. Walter Jacobs Music Publishing Co., 1907. Personal Collection.

"By the Old Oak Tree." Lyrics by George V. Hobart. Music by Max Hoffmann. Pub. Rogers Brothers Music Publishing Co., 1904. *The Rogers Brothers in Paris*. MCNY.

"By the Sycamore Tree." Lyrics by George V. Hobart and Ed Gardenier. Music by Max Hoffmann. Pub. Rogers Brothers Music Publishing Co., 1903. *The Rogers Brothers in London*. MCNY.

"Carmen the Second." Lyrics by Glen McDonough. Music by Raymond Hubbell. Pub. Chas. K. Harris, 1909. *The Midnight Sons*. MCNY.

"The Castle House Rag." Music by James Reese Europe. Pub. Jos. W. Stern and Co., 1914. LC.

"Chick, Chick, Chick." Lyrics by Anne Caldwell. Music by Jerome Kern. Pub. T. B. Harms Co., 1920. *Hitchy-Koo of 1920*. LC.

"The Chicken Coop Girls." Lyrics and music by Harry B. Smith, Robert B. Smith, and Ned Wayburn. Copyright protection copy. CO.

"Chu Chin Chow." Lyrics by Gene Buck. Music by Dave Stamper. Pub. T. B. Harms and Francis, Day, and Hunter, 1917. *Ziegfeld Follies of 1917*. MCNY.

"Come and Dance with Me." Lyrics by Harold Atteridge. Music by Louis A. Hirsch and Melville J. Gideon. Pub. M. Witmark and Sons, 1911. *Vera Violette*. MD–U.C.

"Come to the Moon." Lyrics by Ned Wayburn and Lou Paley. Music by George Gershwin. Pub. T. B. Harms and Francis, Day, and Hunter, 1919. *The Demi-Tasse Revue* (interpolated after opening). CO.

"Dance the Tango With Me." Lyrics and music by Ned Wayburn. Pub. Leo Feist Inc., 1912. CO.

"Dat's the Time You Never Never Never is Around." Lyrics and music by Ned Wayburn. Pub. Wayburn and Co., 1899. Private collection.

"Don't You Wish You were a Kid Again." Lyrics by Gene Buck. Music by Stamper. Pub. T. B. Harms and Francis, Day, and Hunger, 1916. *Ziegfeld Midnight Frolic of 1916*. LC.

"Eily Riley." Lyrics by Glen McDonough. Music by Raymond Hubbell. Pub.

Chas. K. Harris, 1909. *The Midnight Sons*. MCNY.

"Every Girl is Fishing." Lyrics by Gene Buck. Music by Dave Stamper. Pub. T. B. Harms Co., 1916. *Ziegfeld Midnight Frolic of 1916*. LC.

"Everybody Loves a Chicken." Lyrics and music by Bobby Jones. Pub. O'Neill and Story, and T.B. Harms Co., 1912. *Broadway to Paris*. MCNY.

"The Gaby Glide." Lyrics by Harry Pilcer. Music by Edward Eylsler. Copyright protection copy. Shubert Archive.

"Garden of My Dreams." Lyrics by Gene Buck. Music by Louis A. Hirsch and Dave Stamper. Pub. T. B. Harms Co. 1918. *Ziegfeld Follies of 1918*. MCNY.

"The Gertrude Hoffmann Glide." Lyrics and music by Max Hoffmann. Pub. T. B. Harms and Francis, Day and Hunter, and Jerome H. Remick Co., 1912. *Broadway to Paris*. MCNY.

"Golden Evenings of Another Time." Lyrics and music by Herbert Stoddard and Ned Wayburn. Pub. Leo Feist Inc., 1921. *Miss 1917*. CO.

"The Golden Stairs of Love." Lyrics by Harold Atteridge. Music by Jean Schwartz. Pub. Jerome and Schwartz Publishing Co., 1913. *Passing Show of 1912*. MD-U.C.

"The Grizzly Bear." Lyrics by Irving Berlin. Music by George Botsford. Pub. Ted Snyder Co., 1910. *Ziegfeld Follies of 1910*. Private collection.

"Harem Life." Lyrics and music by Irving Berlin. Pub. Irving Berlin Music Publishing Co., 1919. MD.

"Hawaiian Bluebird." Lyrics and music by Carey Morgan, Lew Porter, and Arthur N. Swanstone. Pub. Jos. W. Stern and Co., 1919. MD-U.C.

"Hawaiian Nights." Lyrics and music by Lee B. Roberts. Pub. Robbins Music Corp., 1919. MD-U.C.

"Hawaiian Smiles." Lyrics and music by Mary Earl. Pub. Shapiro, Bernstein and Co., 1919. MD-U.C.

"He Certainly Was Good to Me." Lyrics by Jean Chavez. Music by A.B. Sloan. Pub. William Pilling, 1898. *The Swell Miss Fitzwell*. Private collection.

"Hello Cupid, Send Me a Fellow." Lyrics by Melville Alexander. Music by Anatole Friedland. Pub. Jerome H. Remick and Co., 1912. *Broadway to Paris*. BU.

"Here Come the Yanks with the Tanks." Lyrics and music by Ned Wayburn and Harold Orlob. Pub. Leo Feist Inc., 1918. *Hitchy-Koo of 1918*. CO.

"Honeymoon." Lyrics by Arthur Francis (Ira Gershwin). Music by Paul Lanin. Pub. T. B. Harms and Francis, Day, and Hunter, 1921. *Two Little Girls in Blue*. MCNY.

"How Can You Tell?" Lyrics and music by Ned Wayburn and Harold Orlob. Pub. Leo Feist Inc., 1918. CO.

"Hula Blues." Lyrics by Sonny Cuoha. Music by John A. Noble. Pub. Noble Publishing Co., 1919. MD-U.C.

"I Left Her on the Beach at Honolulu." Lyrics by Gene Buck. Music by Louis A. Hirsch. Pub. T. B. Harms Co., 1916. *Ziegfeld Follies of 1916*. MCNY.

"I Love the Land of Old Black Joe." Lyrics by Grant Clarke. Music by Walter Donaldson. Pub. Irving Berlin Music Publishing Co., 1920. *The Ed Wynn Carnival*. MCNY.

"I Want to Learn How to Jazz Dance." Lyrics by Gene Buck. Music by Dave Stamper. Pub. T. B. Harms and Francis, Day, and Hunger, 1918. *Ziegfeld Follies of 1918*. MCNY.

"I'd Rather See a Minstrel Show." Lyrics and music by Irving Berlin. Pub. Irving

Berlin Music Publishing Co., 1919. *Ziegfeld Follies of 1919.* MCNY.

"If Pavlova Started Buck and Winging." Lyrics by Harold Atteridge. Music by Sigmund Romberg and Louis A. Hirsch. *Show of Wonders of 1916.* Copyright protection copy. Shubert Archive.

"In Monte Carlo Town." Lyrics by Edward Madden. Music by Ben. M. Jerome. Pub. F. B. Haviland of Toronto, 1907. *The Mimic World.* MCNY.

"In the Beautiful Garden of Girls." Lyrics by Gene Buck. Music by Raymond Hubbell. Pub. T. B. Harms and Francis, Day, and Hunter, 1917. *Ziegfeld Follies of 1917.* MD.

"It's Getting Dark on Old Broadway." Lyrics and music by Louis A. Hirsch, Gene Buck, and Dave Stamper. Pub. T. B. Harms Co., 1922. *Ziegfeld Follies of 1922.* BU.

"I've Got No Use for a Fighting Man." Lyrics and music by Ned Wayburn. Pub. Wayburn and Co., 1899. Private collection.

"I've Got Rings on My Fingers." Lyrics by Weston Barnes. Music by Maurice Scott. Pub. T. B. Harms and Francis, Day, and Hunter, 1909. *The Midnight Sons.* MCNY.

"I've Said Goodbye to Broadway." Lyrics by Gene Buck. Music by Dave Stamper. Pub. T. B. Harms and Francis, Day, and Hunter, 1916. *Ziegfeld Follies of 1916.* BU.

"Just a Kiss (The Raffles Dance)." Lyrics and music by Bobby Jones. Pub. O. E. Story, 1913. *Broadway to Paris.* LC.

"The Land Where the Good Songs Go." Lyrics by P. G. Wodehouse. Music by Jerome Kern. Pub. T. B. Harms Co., 1917. *Miss 1917.* LC.

"Luana Lou." Lyrics by Gene Buck. Music by Dave Stamper. Pub. T. B. Harms Co., 1919. *Ziegfeld Midnight Frolic of 1916.* LC.

"The Maiden with the Dreamy Eyes." Lyrics by James Weldon Johnson. Music by Bob Cole. Pub. Jos. W. Stern and Co., 1901. *The Hall of Fame.* MCNY.

"The Melting Pot." Lyrics by Gene Buck. Music by Dave Stamper. Pub. T. B. Harms and Francis, Day, and Hunter, 1916. *Ziegfeld Midnight Frolic of 1916.* LC.

"My American Beauty Rose." Lyrics by Gene Buck. Music by Dave Stamper. Pub. T. B. Harms Co., 1916. *Ziegfeld Midnight Frolic of 1916.* LC.

"My Baby's Arms." Lyrics by Joseph McCarthy. Music by Harry Tierney. Pub. Leo Feist Inc., 1919. *Ziegfeld Follies of 1919.* MCNY.

"My Lady of the Nile." Lyrics by Gene Buck. Music by Jerome Kern. Pub. T. B. Harms Co., 1916. *Ziegfeld Follies of 1916.* MCNY.

"My Little Chick." Lyrics by George Totten Smith. Music by Ned Wayburn. Pub. Sol Bloom, 1904. *Ned Wayburn's Girls of 1904.* LC.

"My Little Havana Maid." Lyrics by Bert Ellis. Music by Anatole Friedland. Pub. Leo Feist Inc., 1910. *The Wife Hunters.* Shubert Archive.

"My Rag-Time Queen." Lyrics and music by Ned Wayburn. Private collection.

"My Sahara Rose." Lyrics by Grant Clarke. Music by Walter Donaldson. Pub. Irving Berlin Publishing Corp., 1920. *The Ed Wynn Carnival.* MCNY.

"My Sist' Tetrazzini." Lyrics by Edward Madden. Music by Anatole Friedland after Mascagni. Pub. Trebuhs Publishing Co., 1909. *The Midnight Sons.* MCNY.

"My Sweet." Lyrics by William Jerome. Music by Jean Schwartz. Pub. Jerome H. Remick and Co., 1905. *The Rain-dears.* (Originally written for *In Tammany Hall*.) BU.

"Neath the South Sea Moon." Lyrics and music by Gene Buck, Louis A. Hirsch, and Dave Stamper. Pub. T. B. Harms Co., 1922. *Ziegfeld Follies of 1922.* MCNY.

"Nijinsky." Lyrics by Gene Buck. Music by Dave Stamper. Pub. T. B. Harms and Francis, Day, and Hunter, 1916. *Ziegfeld Follies of 1916.* LC.

"Oh Me! Oh My!" Lyrics by Arthur Francis. Music by Vincent Youmans. Pub. T. B. Harms and Francis, Day, and Hunter, 1921. *Two Little Girls in Blue.* MCNY.

"Oh! Mr. Moon." Lyrics and music by George M. Cohan. Pub. Mill Publishing Co., 1901. *The Governor's Son.* MCNY.

"Old Folks at Home." Lyrics and music by Stephen Collins Foster. Arrangement by Percy Weinrich, 1904. Pub. McKinley Music Co., 1905. MD-P.I.

"On San Francisco Bay." Lyrics by Vincent Bryan. Music by Gertrude Hoffmann. Pub. M. Witmark and Sons and Jerome H. Remick and Co., 1906. *The Parisian Model.* Private collection.

"The Palm Beach Dip." Lyrics by Stanley Murphy. Music by Harry Tierney. Pub. Jerome H. Remick and Co., 1918. *Miss 1917.* LC.

"Paree's a Branch of Broadway." Lyrics and music by Max Hoffmann. Pub. T. B. Harms and Francis, Day, and Hunter, 1912. *Broadway to Paris.* LC.

"Peaches." Lyrics by P. G. Wodehouse. Music by Jerome Kern. Pub. T. B. Harms Co., 1917. *Miss 1917.* LC.

"The Picture I Want to See." Lyrics by P. G. Wodehouse. Music by Jerome Kern. Pub. T. B. Harms Co., 1917. *Miss 1917.* LC.

"Pocahontas." Lyrics and music by Gus Edwards. Pub. Gus Edwards Music Publishing Co., 1905. *The Daisy Dancers.* BU.

"Rag-Time Jimmie's Jamboree." Lyrics and music by Ned Wayburn. Pub. Wayburn and Co., 1899. Shubert Archive.

"The Pony Ballet Girl." Lyrics and music by Irene Franklyn and Burt Green. Pub. Leo Feist Inc., 1909. MD-U.C.

"Rambler Rose." Lyrics and music by Louis A. Hirsch, Gene Buck, and Dave Stamper. Pub. T. B. Harms Co., 1922. *Ziegfeld Follies of 1922.* MD.

"Sahara—Soon We'll Be Dry Like You." Lyrics by Harold Atteridge. Music by Sigmund Romberg. Pub. Jerome H. Remick and Co., 1919. *Monte Christo, Jr..* MD.

"Shake Your Feet." Lyrics by Gene Buck. Music by Dave Stamper. Pub. T. B. Harms Co., 1923. *Ziegfeld Follies of 1923.* MCNY.

"She's a Thoroughbred." Lyrics and music by Ned Wayburn. Pub. *New York Journal Musical Supplement,* 25 Dec. 1898. BU.

"Sonambulistic Tune." Lyrics by Gene Buck. Music by Dave Stamper. Pub. T. B. Harms and Francis, Day, and Hunger, 1916. *Ziegfeld Follies of 1916.* BU.

"The Spaniard that Blighted My Life." Lyrics and music by Billy Merson. Pub. T. B. Harms and Francis, Day, and Hunter, 1911. *The Honeymoon Express.* MCNY.

"Spend Your Money While You Live." Lyrics and music by Ned Wayburn. Pub. Wayburn and Co., 1899. Private collection.

"Starlight." Lyrics by Gene Buck. Music by Dave Stamper. Pub. T. B. Harms and Francis, Day, and Hunter, 1918. *Ziegfeld Follies of 1918.* MD.

"Swanee." Lyrics by Irving Caesar. Music by George Gershwin. Pub. Leo Feist Inc., 1919. *The Demi-Tasse Revue.* MCNY (filed as *Sinbad Jr.*).

"Swanee River Blues." Lyrics by Gene Buck. Music by Dave Stamper. Pub. T. B.

Harms Co., 1923. *Ziegfeld Follies of 1923.* MCNY.

"Syncopated Sandy." Lyrics and music by Ned Wayburn and Stanley Whiting. Pub. Broder and Schlam, 1897. BU.

"Syncopatia Land." Lyrics by Harold Atteridge. Music by Jean Schwartz. Pub. Jean Schwartz Music Publishing Co., 1913. *The Honeymoon Express.* MCNY.

"Teaching the Baby to Walk." Lyrics by Ned Wayburn. Music by Harold Orlob. Pub. T. B. Harms Co., 1921. *Town Gossip.* MD.

"That Mysterious Rag." Lyrics and music by Irving Berlin and Ted Snyder. Pub. Ted Snyder Co. Music Publishers, 1911. LC.

"There Must Be a Girl for Me Somewhere." Lyrics by William LeBaron. Music by Ned Wayburn. Pub. Leo Feist Inc., 1912. CO.

"There's Ragtime in the Air." Lyrics by Gene Buck. Music by Dave Stamper. Pub. T. B. Harms Co., 1916. *Ziegfeld Follies of 1916.* LC.

"Trouble Never Troubles This Coon." Lyrics and music by Ned Wayburn. Pub. Wayburn and Co., 1899. *The Sunday Examiner Musical Supplement*, n.d. BU.

"Tulip Time." Lyrics by Gene Buck. Music by Dave Stamper. Pub. T. B. Harms Co., 1919. *Ziegfeld Follies of 1919.* MCNY.

"Turkey Trot." Lyrics and music by Joseph M. Daly. Pub. Joseph M. Daly Music Publishers, 1912. Private collection.

"The Wedding Glide." Lyrics and music by Louis A. Hirsch. Pub. Shapiro Music Publishing Co., 1912. *Passing Show of 1912.* LC.

"When Charlie Plays the Slide Trombone in the Silver Cornet Band." Lyrics by George V. Hobart. Music by Mae A. Sloane. Pub. Jos. W. Stern, 1902. *The Hall of Fame.* MCNY.

"When Gaby Did the Gaby Glide." Lyrics by Harold Atteridge. Music by Jean Schwartz. Pub. Jean Schwartz Music Publishing Co., 1913. *The Honeymoon Express.* Shubert Archive.

"When It's Apple Blossom Time in Normandy." Lyrics and music by Nora Bayes and Jack Norwith. Pub. Bayes and Norwith Music Publishing Co., 1912. *The Sun Dodgers.* MCNY.

"When the Lights are Low." Lyrics by Gene Buck. Music by Jerome Kern. Pub. T. B. Harms Co., 1916. *Ziegfeld Follies of 1916.* MCNY.

"When They're Old Enough to Know Better, It's Better to Leave Them Alone." Lyrics by Sam M. Lewis and Joe Young. Music by Harry Ruby. *Ziegfeld Follies of 1919.* Columbia Records Social Projects, Smithsonian Collection, #P14272, Side One, cut 4.

"When Uncle Sam is Ruler of the Sea." Lyrics by Henry Blossom. Music by Victor Herbert. Pub. T. B. Harms and Francis, Day, and Hunter, 1916. *The Century Girl.* BU.

"When Was There Ever a Night Like This?" Lyrics and music by Louis A. Hirsch. Pub. Shapiro Music Publishing Co., 1912. *Passing Show of 1912.* MCNY.

"Who Paid the Rent for Mrs. Rip van Winkle When Rip van Winkle was Asleep?" Lyrics and music by Alfred Bryan and Fred Fisher. Pub. Leo Feist Inc., 1914. *The Honeymoon Express.* MCNY.

"Why Do They Die at the End of a Classical Dance?" Lyrics by William Jerome and Alex Gerber. Music by Jean Schwartz. Pub. M. Witmark and Sons, 1921. *The Rose of Stamboul.* Shubert Archive.

"Will O'The Wisp." Lyrics by Gene Buck. Music by Stamper. Pub. T. B. Harms Co., 1916. *Ziegfeld Midnight Frolic of 1916.* LC.

"The Yankee Boy in Blue." Lyrics by Edward Madden. Music by Dorothy Jardon. Pub. Jerome H. Remick and Co., 1907. *The Daisy Dancers*. BU.

"You Cannot Make Your Shimmy Shake on Tea." Lyrics and music by Irving Berlin. Pub. Irving Berlin Music Publishing Co., 1919. *Ziegfeld Follies of 1919*. MCNY.

"You're a Perfect Jewel to Me!" Lyrics by Gene Buck. Music by Dave Stamper. Pub. T. B. Harms Co., 1919. *Ziegfeld Midnight Frolic*. LC.

Published Song Anthologies

Charters, Ann, ed. *The Ragtime Songbook*. New York: Oak Publications, 1965.

Gottschalk, Louis Moreau. *Piano Works of Louis Moreau Gottschalk*. New York: Arno Press, 1970.

Hosfeld, Samuel. *The Minstrel*. Philadelphia: J.W. Pepper, 1883.

Lamb, Joseph F. *Ragtime Treasures and Piano Solos by Joseph F. Lamb*. Melville, N.Y.: Belwin/Mills Publishing, 1964.

Lawrence, Vera Brodsky, ed. *The Collected Works of Scott Joplin*. New York: New York Public Library, 1971.

Morath, Max, ed. *Guide to Ragtime: A Collection of Ragtime Songs and Piano Solos*. New York: Hollis Music, 1964.

Renoa, Kapulé. *Collection of Native Hawaiian Songs and Hulas*. New York: J. Franklyn Music Corp., 1913.

Lyrics Without Extant Music

Atteridge, Harold, *et al. Collection of Uncredited Songs Lyrics from Shows Produced by Messrs. J. J. and Lee Shubert*, ca. 1912–1919. Bound typescript. Shubert Archive.

Wayburn, Ned, *et al. The Delaney Song-Book*, ca. 1893–1925. Special Collections, Music Division, New York Public Library for the Performing Arts.

Music Without Extant Lyrics

Hoffmann, Max, Fred Solomon, *et al.* Manuscript arrangements of original and extant songs, ca.1893–1920. Private collection.

Hoffmann, Max, Fred Solomon, Percy Weinrigh, *et al.* Manuscript and published arrangements of extant songs, ca. 1893–1920. Special Collections, Music Division, New York Public Library for the Performing Arts.

Friedland, Anatole, *et al.* Manuscript orchestral scores for *The Wife Hunters*, ca. 1911. Shubert Archive.

Hirsch, Louis A., *et al.* Manuscript orchestral scores for the *Passing Show of 1912*. ca. 1911–1912. Private collection.

_____. Manuscript orchestral scores for the *Passing Show of 1913*. ca. 1912–1913. Shubert Archive.

Romberg, Sigmund. Manuscript piano scores for shows produced at the Winter Garden Theatre by J. J. and Lee Shubert, ca. 1913–1920. Music Division, Library of Congress.

Adelaide and Hughes, 44, 46
Albee, Edward Franklyn, *12*
American Piano Company (Ampico), 82
Anderson, F. Richard, 10
Anderson, John Murray, 11
Allan, Maud, 58, 70
Astaire, Adele, 62
Astaire, Fred, xiii, 13, 43, 62
Atteridge, Harold, 36, 48, 61, 71
Aymar, Neva, 23, 24

Bacon, Virginia, *17*
Ballets: *L'Après-midi d'un Faune*, 36;
    Autumn Bacchanale, 35; *Petrouchka*, 36;
    Schéhérazade, 35-36; *Le Spectre de la*
    Rose, 35; *Les Sylphides*, 35, 36, 68
Ballets Russes, 35, 36, 68
Bankoff, Ivan, 16
Barclay, Don, 34
Belasco, David, 34, 40
Berkeley, Busby, 61
Berlin, Irving, 48, 69
Blume, Norman, 34
Boggs, Esther, 28
Boley, May, 38
Bonner, Mabel, 28
Booth, Edwin, 2
Bordoni, Madame, 38
Brice, Fanny, 35-36, 48, 68, 69
Broun, Heywood, 70
Buck, Gene, 35, 49, 61
Burrows-Fontaine, Evan, 48, 55

Caesar, Irving, 61
Caldwell, Anne, 61
Cantor, Eddie, xi, 49, 71
Carroll, Earl, 56, 61, 72
Carus, Emma, 22
Castle, Vernon, 44; and Irene, 36
Ceballos, Hilarion, 23, 24, 46
Ceballos, Larry, 60
Ceballos, Rosalia, 23, 24, 33, *34*, 46
Cellarius, Henri, 7
Chautauqua Lyceum, 4
Chauve-Souris, 70
Chicago Musical College, 2, 4
Chicago School of Elocution. *See* Hart
    Conway School of Acting

Chicago Training School, 1
Claire, Ina, 49
Clayton, Bessie, 18, 37-38, 40
Cochran, Hal, 82
Cohan, George M., 44, 70, 73
Cole, Bob, 24, 28, 61
Connolly, Bobby, 61
Connor Twins, 58
Conway, Alice Brooks, 2
Conway, Hart, 1-2, 3
Conway Conservatory of Dramatic Art.
    See Hart Conway School of Acting
Cosmopolitan Pictures, 13
Costume, 22, 25, 26, 29-31, 51-52, 56, 57,
    65-66
Courville, Albert de, 11, 41
Cross, Wellington, 37, 38-40, 44, 46

Daly, Augustin, 64-65
Dance Masters of America, 82
Dances:
  Black Bottom, 18; Castle Walk, 18;
    Charleston, 18, 102-105; cotillion, 7-8,
    9, 10; Gaby Glide, 35, 43, 44, 45;
    Gertrude Hoffmann Glide, 44-45;
    Grizzly Bear, 18, 49; glide, 18, 44-45;
    hesitation, 18, 44; hula, 15, 48-50, 52, 55;
    "La Java," 49; *kazachok*, 16, 44, 70;
    maxixe, 18; one-step, 18, 42, 43, 49;
    Savannah Stomp, 100-101; shimmy, 49;
    tango, 18, 42, 43; Turkey Trot, 18, 45;
    two-step, 18;
  aerial, 19, 33, 65, 73; apache, 46, 70;
    Arabian, 48, 52, 55; "boat deck," 17, 40;
    "chair," *23*, 53, 71; dervish, 38; "doll,"
    15, 16, 72; "drunk," 16, 17, 40, 44;
    flirtation, 54; mirror, 40, 46-47, 50;
    nautch, 38; precision, 52, 53-54; "rube,"
    43, 44; shadow, 40, 46-47; "soldier," 15,
    16, 52, 54; tandem, 40, *41*, 42, 45, 46-47,
    50; whirlwind, 42, 45-46
d'Auban, Ernest, 11, 65, 73
Davis, Josephine, 22
de Haven, Carter, 37, 40, *41*, 42
Delsarte, François, 3, 4-5, 8, 30
Denver Conservatory of the Arts, 4
Deslys, Gaby, 43, 45, 70
Dillingham, Charles B., 11, *12*

Dolly Sisters, 50, 55

Dolores, 58, *59*

Donahue, Jack, 43-44, *43*, *47*, 48

Dougherty, Byrd, 24

Drills, 3, 7; aesthetic drills, 8; fan drills, 10, 30; fancy drills, 8-10; flag drills, 10, 30; military drills, 6

Duff-Gordon, Lady (Lucile), 57

Eaton, Pearl, 61

Edwards, Gus, 24, 28

Erlanger, A[braham] L[incoln], x, 10, *12*. *See also* Klaw and Erlanger

Erté, *72*

Evans, Arthur, 61

Fairbanks Twins (also known as Thankhauser Twins), 46-47, *47*

Falk, Eleanor, 22

Famous Player-Laskey Films, 12

Fanchon and Marco, 11, 60

Fields, Lew, 11, 33, 37, 44, 69

Fields, W. C., xi, 12, 35

Fokine, Michel, 35

Frances, Corene, 37

Friedland, Anatole, 61

Friganza, Trixie, 34, 51

Gambarelli, Maria, 11

Gates, Eleanor, 34

Gaynor, William Jay, 40

Genée, Adeline, 34

Gershwin, George, 61

Gershwin, Ira, 47, 61

Gilbert and Sullivan, 36

Glazunov, Alexander, 35

Goldwyn, Samuel. *See* Samuel Goldwyn Productions

Granville, Barnard, 49

Gray, Gilda, 49, 50, 55, 62, 71

Greenwood, Charlotte, 37, 38

Gresham, Herbert, 11, 64-65, 73, 74

Gros, Ernest M., 28

Haggin, Ben Ali, 11, 66

Haig, Emma, 35

Hale, Chester, 11, 60, 61

Hammerstein, Oscar, 40; and William, 10, 21, 22, 23

Hardy, Sam B., 35, 68

Hart Conway School of Acting, 1, 2, 3, 4, 10

Hatzfeldt, Olga von (Countess), 22

Hay, Mary, 43

Headline Vaudeville Production Company, 11, 15, 21, 23, 25, 28, 65, 66

Herbert, Victor, 61

Herron, Bertie, 25

Hirsch, Louis A., 34, 35, 37, 49

Hoff, Vanda, 38, 47, 48

Hoffmann, Gertrude (stage name of Kitty Hayes), ix, 10, 11, 34, 44, 58, 61, 68

Hoffmann, Max ("Baron"), 10, 24, 61, 66

Hopkins, John (Colonel), 10

Huffman, J.C., 76

Irwin, May, 10

Jacobsen, C. H. (Karl Heinrich), 2

Jardon, Dorothy, 24, 28, 29, 31, 32, 61

Jerome, William, 24, 28, 30

Johns, Al, 24

Johnson, J. Rosamond, 24, 28, 61

Jolson, Al, xi, 70, 71

Josephine, Lois, 37, 38-40, 44, 46

Keith Vaudeville Circuit, 10, 23

Keith-Albee-Orpheum Theater Circuit, 12

Kern, Jerome, 61

Kessner, Della, 28

King, Mazie, 18, 34, 38, *39*, 42, 69

King of Jazz, The, 61

Kiralfy Brothers, 65

Klaw, Marc, x, 10. *See also* Klaw and Erlanger

Klaw and Erlanger, 10, 21, 22, 23; School of Stage Dancing, 22, 28

Kosloff, Alexis, 82

Kosloff, Theodore, 68

Lamaedrid, Julia, 28, *29*

Langstaff, A.M., 28

Lannin, Paul, 61

Law, Evelyn, 13, 15, *15*, 43-44, *43*, 47, 61

Lederer, George, 65

Leonidoff, Leon, 60

Ling, Per Henrik (system of gymnastics), 2, 3, 65

Lonergan, John, 61

Lorraine, Lillian, 47

MacFadden, Byrne, 50

MacKaye, Hazel, 36

MacKaye, Steele, 4

Madame Butterfly, 30

Madden, Edward, 24, 28

Marlowe, Dorothy, 65

Meeker, Mabel, 34

Mendelssohn, Felix, 10, 58
Merrill, Blanche, 48, 61, 69
Metro-Goldwyn-Mayer (MGM), 12
Miller, Marilyn, 62
Mitchell, Julian, 57
Modjeska, Helena, 2
Monroe, George, 37, 69
Monstery, T[homas] H[oyer] (Colonel), 2–3, 6, 8
Moon, George, 34
Moon and Morris, 46
Moore, Gladys, 18, 34
Mordkin, Mikhail, 35, 68
Morgan, Anna, 4
Morse, Theodore F., 24, 26
Mouvet, Maurice, 34, 70

National American Suffrage Association, 36
Newspapers and magazines, *Dance Lovers Magazine*, 50; *The Dance Magazine*, 82; *The Graphic*, 42; *Green Book*, 55; *Life Magazine*, 56; *New York Globe*, 47; *New York Morning Telegraph*, 42; *New York Tribune*, 5; *The Theatre Magazine*, 21; *Variety*, 54
Nice, Fred, Jr., 37, 40, *41*, 42
Nichols, Nellie V., 22
Nijinsky, Vaslav, 35, 36, 68

O. B. Howell's Conservatory of Music, 4
O'Denishawn, Florence, 48
Offenbach, Jacques, 58
Original English Pony Ballet, 15, 25, 31, 33, 46, 53, 65, 66

Pankhurst, Emmeline, 37, 69
Paramount-Publix Corporation, 12
Paris Exposition (1900), 38
Parker, Flora, 40
Partington, Jack, 11
Pavlova, Anna, 34, 35, 51, 52, 68
Pennington, Ann, 15, 49, 50, 55, 62
Petroff, Boris, 11
Phillips, Cole, 56, 72
Pilcer, Harry, 23, 24, 26, 43, 45, 61
Plays and shows (other than by Wayburn), *The Allegory*, 36; *The Bird of Paradise*, 49; *Bought and Paid For*, 34; *The Casino Girl*, 15; *Frou Frou*, 2; *Julius Caesar*, 37; *King Lear*, 2; *Kismet*, 34, 71; *Monte Christo, Jr.*, 71; *Parsafalia*, 22; *Poor Little Rich Girl*, 34; *The Return of Peter Grimm*, 34; *Sumurun*, 34; *The Swell Miss Fitzwell*, 10; *Tales of Hoffmann*,

58; *Vera Violette*, 45, 70; *The Wall Street Girl*, 70
Porter, Zadora, 28
Proctor Vaudeville Chain, 23, 28
Prologs, 11-12, 60-61
Puccini, Giacomo, 30
Pulley, Luke, 22

Quinault, Robert, 72

Randall, Carl, 35
Rasch, Albertina, 61
Remick, Jerome H., 31, 67
Rogers, Ginger, 43
Rogers, Will, xi, 30
Romberg, Sigmund, 61, 71
Romeo, Vincenzo, 69
Rupp, Carl, 82

St. Denis, Ruth, 48, 70, 82
Samuel Goldwyn Productions, 13
Sanger, Hazel, 28
Saye, Agnes, 7, 10, 73
Schaall, Ida, 51
Schwartz, Jean, 24, 28, 30, 61
Serven, Winfield S., 4
Shakespeare, William, 37
Shawn, Ted, 48, 82
Sheriffe, Hadji, 38
Shubert Brothers, x, 11, 33
Simpson-Serven, Ida, xii, 2, 3, 5
Singer, Mortimer, 11
Singer Midgets, 77
Solar, Willie, 42
Solomon, Fred, 10, 24, 28
Songs:
   "Arabian Songs," 71; "Becky Songs," 48, 69; "Sadie Songs," 48, 69, 71;
   Titles: "A Pretty Girl is Like a Melody," 57, 58; "Aloha Ai," 49; "The Bacchanale Rag," 34-35, 36, 45; "The Ballet Girl," "The Beautiful Garden of Girls," 57; "Beautiful Girls," 57; "Beautiful Jewel," 58; "Becky from Babylon," 69; "Becky is Back in the Ballet," 69; "Bring on the Girls," 58; "Daisyland" (also "Daisy"), 28, 30; "Dearest," 58; "Dixie," 26; "Every Girl is Doing Her Bit," 54; "Footloose," 82; "The Gaby Glide," 70; "I Left Her on the Beach at Honolulu," 49; "Luana Lou," 49; "Mexico" ("Fandango Fanny"), 28, 67; "My Little Lady of Japan," 28, 30; "'Neath the South Sea Moon," 49; "Nijinsky," 36;

"Pocohontas," 28, 29-30; "Sadie Salome, Go Home," 48; "Sahara—Soon We'll Be Dry Like You," 71; "The Surprise Package," 54; "Swanee," 61; "When Gaby Did the Gaby Glide," 45, 70; "The Yankee Boy in Blue," 28, 31; "You Don't Need the Wine to Have a Wonderful Time, When They Still Make Those Beautiful Girls," 57

Sparling, Cleo, 28
Stamper, Dave, 49, 61
Stanwyck, Barbara, 62
Stebbins, Genevieve, 4
Steele, John, 49, 58
Stewart, Anita, 13
Sunshine, Marion, 53

Tanguay, Eva, 45, 70
Tascott, 22
Theaters:
  Chicago: Bijou Opera Company, 1; Chicago Grand Opera House, 1; Chicago Museum, 1; Lyceum Theater, 1; Middleton's West Side Museum, 1; Olympia Theater, 1; State Street (Hopkins) Theater, 10;
  London: Hippodrome, 11, 33, 41; Middlesex Music Halls, 11; Palladium, 11;
  New York: Capitol Theater, 12, 31, 60, 61, 79; Century Theater, 11; Crystal Garden Theater, 21; Hippodrome, 54; New Amsterdam, 57; New Amsterdam Roof Theater, 56; New York Theater, 10, 22; New York Theater Roof, 21, 33; Paradise Garden Roof Theater, 21, 22; Proctor's 23rd Street Theater, 28; Radio City Music Hall, 60, 61; Roxy Theater, 60; Winter Garden Theater, 36, 69;
  Other: Proctor Theater (Troy, N.Y.), 28
Tiller, John, 15, 65
Tilzer, Harry von, 24
Towson Twins, 47
Twin acts, 46-47. See also Connor Twins, Fairbanks Twins, Towson Twins

University of Denver, 4
Urban, Joseph, 5, 6, 49, 54, 56, 57, 71
Uzell, Corene, 28, 29

Vitak, Albertina, 61
Voegtlin, Arthur, 33
Walker, Aida Overton, ix

Walton, Florence, 34, 70
Wayburn, Ned,
  Education and early career, 1-10;
  Choreography: chorus divisions, 18-20, 51-57; chorus formations, 18; 24-26, 41, 42, 52-53, 55, 58-59; dance instructions, 82-106; influence of, 60-62; influences on, 3, 4-5, 6-7, 8, 10; insertion technique, 33, 42-50; montage technique, 33-42, 58; processionals, 56-58; routine format, 6-7, 50; Ziegfeld Walk, 5, 55-56;
  Dance techniques and modes: acrobatic, 16-17, *23*, 58, 98-99; ballroom, 18, 42, 82, 103-105; characterizational, 15, 16, 40, 42-46, 55; eccentric, 14-15, 16, 17-18, *39*, 40, 43, 48; foundation, 84-90; legomania, 16; modern Americanized ballet, 17-18, 58, 59, 91-97; musical comedy, 14-15, 16, 53, 54, 55, 58; "Russian" (Cossack) tap, 16; tap (tapping and stepping), 14, 15-16, 47, 52, 53, 55, 58, 86-90, 100-101; toe, 18-19; toe tapping ("trick" ballet), 18, 37-38;
  Teaching, x-xi, 3, *3*, 5, 82;
  Works:
    Feature acts, 21-32; *The Daisy Dancers*, 10, 23, 24, 28-32, *29*; *The Futurity Winner*, 23; *Ned Wayburn's Girlie Gambols*, 49; *Ned Wayburn's Minstrel Misses*, x, 7, 26, *27*; *The Phantastic Phantoms*, 23, *23*, 24, 46; *The Rain-dears*, 23, 24, 25, 26, 28, 31; *The Side Show*, 23, 24, 25-26; *The Star Bout*, 23; *The Sunny South*, 22, 24; *The Three CH's (CHic, CHarm and CHaste)*, 25; Films: xiii; *The Great White Way*, 13, 61; *Potash and Perlmutter*, 13, 61; Prologs, 11-12, 13; *The Demi-Tasse Revue*, 12, 26, 31, 66; *Makin' Believe*, 46; *Ned Wayburn's Ritz Revue*, 79; *Ned Wayburn's Song Scenes*, 12, 26; Scenes: "Awakening of the Daisies," 31; "The Bacchanale Rag," 35, 44, 52; "The Blushing Ballet," 34, 35-36, 68; "Broadway Indians," "The Capitol Steps," 11, 36-42; "The Chicken Coop Rag," 55; "The Chicken Rag," 55; "Dinjies," "Escalade, or the Magic Staircase," 11, 33, 41-42; "Everybody Loves a Chicken," 55; "Every Girl is Fishing," 54; "Follies Salad," 47; "The Galli-Curci Rag," 44; "Harem Scene,"

34, 35, 51-52; "A Hawaiian Tourist," 49; "Hello Cub, Send Me A Fellow," 53; "I Left Her on the Beach in Honolulu," 50; "In Daisyland," 28, 30-31; "In Old Japan," 10, 28, 30, 31; "In Old Mexico," 28-29, *29*, 31; "In Old Virginia," 28, 29-30, 31; "It's Getting Darker on Broadway," x, 55; "The Jockey Club," 25; "Knitting Dance," 54; "Laceland," 33, 55, 58-59; "Luana Lou," 49-50; "A Miniature," 47, *47*; "My Little Havana Made," 51, *52*; "My Sist' Tetrazzini," 44; "'Neath the South Sea Moon," 49, 53; "North and South," 31; "The Picnic March," 31; "Rambler Rose," *15*; "Say it with Flowers," 31; "Tulip Time," 55, 72; "When Uncle Sam is the Ruler of the Waves," 54; "Will O'The Wisp," 55; Shows: *Broadway to Paris*, 11, 34, 44, 53, 55; *By the Sad Sea Waves*, 10; *The Century Girl*, 11, 54; *The Ed Wynn Carnival*, 11, 48; *Hitchy-Koo of 1920*, 48; *The Honeymoon Express*, 45, 70; *The Jolly Bachelors*, 46; *The Midnight Sons*, 20, 33-34, *34*, 42, 67-68; *The Mimic World*, 11, 20; *Mlle. Mischief*, 11; *Mr. Bluebeard*, 15; *Miss 1917*, 11, 72; *Ned Wayburn's Girls of 1904*, 22, 26, 31, 33; *The Never Homes*, 55; *The Night of the Fourth*, 10; *The Passing Show of 1912*, x, 11, 34, 44, 46, 51-52, 56; *The Passing Show of 1913*, 11, 33, 36-42, 69; *The Pearl and the Pumpkin*, 7; *The Poor Little Ritz Girl*, 11; *Smiles*, 13; *Town Topics*, 11, 26, 43, 44, 53, 55, 66; *Two Little Girls in Blue*, 11, 43-44, *43*, 46, 48, 61; *The Wife Hunters*, 31, 51; *Ziegfeld Follies of 1916*, 11, 34, 35-36, 49, 71; *1917*, 11, 46, 47, 58; *1918*, 11, 46, 47, *47*, 70; *1919*, 11, 46, 47, 55, 58; *1922*, 7, 11, 12, *15*, 20, 30, 33, 49, 53, 54-55, *57*, 58, 71; *1923*, 7, 12; *Ziegfeld Midnight Frolics*, x, 11, 30, 49, 50, 54, 55, 56, 57, 58, *59*; *Zig-Zag*, 54;

Webb, Clifton, 43, 62
Weeks, Ada May, 16, 40
West, Mae, 62
Weyburn, Chauncy, 1
Weyburn, Elbert Delos, 1
Weyburn, Edward Claudius. *See* Wayburn, Ned
Weyburn, Edward Claudius, Jr., 63
Weyburn, Frank, 1
Wheaton, Anna, 34, 52
White, Frances, 54
White, George, 61-62
Whiteman, Paul, 61
Williams, Bert, 35, 68
Wilson, Marie, 47
Wilson, Woodrow, 36
Wood, Swan, 37

Youmans, Vincent, 61

Ziegfeld, William, 2, 11
Ziegfeld, Jr., Florenz, x, 2, 11, 13, 20, 55, 57
Ziegfeld, Sr., Florenz, 2

STUDIES IN DANCE HISTORY is a monographic series published semiannually by the Society of Dance History Scholars on the history of dance and related disciplines. International in outlook, the series is an important forum for research throughout the field as well as a source of long out-of-print classics. Lively, informative, and generously illustrated, STUDIES IN DANCE HISTORY offers a body of scholarly writing that no one seriously interested in dance can do without.

Editorial inquiries and submissions: Judith C. Bennahum, Department of Theatre and Dance, Fine Arts Center, University of New Mexico, Albuquerque, NM 87131.

Subscriptions, back issues, changes of address: Marge Maddux, Dance Program, University of Minnesota, 108 Norris Hall, 172 Pillsbury Drive, S.E., Minnepolis, MN 55455; FAX 612-625-2849; PHONE 612-626-7211.

Subscription price is $45/year or $80 for two years. Postage outside North America is an additional $10/year or $20 for two years. The single copy price is $21.95. Postage and handling rates are $5 for the first book and $3 for each additional book in North America; elsewhere, $5 for the first book and $3 for each additional book. All orders must be prepaid in U.S. funds. Checks should be made out to the Society of Dance History Scholars and sent to Marge Maddux, Dance Program, University of Minnesota, 108 Norris Hall, 172 Pillsbury Drive, S.E., Minneapolis, MN 55455.

European distributor: Dance Books Limited, 9 Cecil Court, London WC2N 4EZ, United Kingdom. Single copy price is £12.50 inland and £15 overseas.

STUDIES IN DANCE HISTORY

Titles in Series Vol. 1, No. 1 Tamiris in Her Own Voice

Vol. 1, No. 2 The Playford Ball

Vol. 2, No. 1 Théleur's Letters on Dancing

Vol. 2, No. 2 The Technique of Martha Graham

Vol. 3, No. 1 The Diaries of Marius Petipa

Vol. 3, No. 2 Looking at Ballet: Ashton and Balanchine, 1926–1936

Vol. 4, No. 1 The Origins of the Bolero School

Vol. 4, No. 2 Carlo Blasis in Russia

Vol. 5, No. 1 Of, By, and For the People: Dancing on the Left in the 1930s

Vol. 5, No. 2 Dancing in Montreal: Seeds of a Choreographic History

New Series: No. 11 Balanchine Pointework

No. 12 The Making of a Choreographer: Ninette de Valois and *Bar aux Folies-Bergère*

No. 13 Ned Wayburn and the Dance Routine: From Vaudeville to the *Ziegfeld Follies*